The Recipe for Success

The Recipe for Success

What really successful people do and how you can do it too

Blaire Palmer

A & C Black • London

First published in Great Britain 2009

A & C Black Publishers Ltd
36 Soho Square, London W1D 3QY
www.acblack.com

Copyright © Blaire Palmer, 2009

A CIP record for this book is available from the British Library.

ISBN: 9–781–4081–0506–1

This book is produced using paper that is made from wood grown in managed,
sustainable forests. It is natural, renewable and recyclable. The logging and
manufacturing processes conform to the environmental regulations of the
country of origin.

Design by Fiona Pike, Pike Design, Winchester
Typeset by RefineCatch Limited, Bungay, Suffolk
Printed and bound in Great Britain by Cox & Wyman, Reading, RG1 8EX

Contents

Acknowledgements

I am very grateful to a large number of people who have helped me with this book. Particular thanks go to my experts – Oli Barrett, Carole Blake, Sharon Connolly, Vicki Day, Lucy Harris, Deborah Meredith, John Savage and Phil Taylor. They gave a great deal of time throughout the process in addition to their insights and practical ideas.

Thank you also to Nelisha Wickremasinghe, Mark West and Lisa Derbyshire for access to their network as well as their support and friendship. Thank you to my own Kitchen Cabinet – Heather Beresford, Mike Wilsher, Graham Massey, Jennifer Chevalier, John Barnes, Ros Munton and Julia Blower – who have helped me think through the recipe for success and run my various theories past them at length.

I could not have written this book without my agent Charlotte Howard, my editor Lisa Carden or my au pair Stephanie Schliecker. Final thanks go to my family: my Mum and Dad, sister Lindsey and daughter Ivy Belle who was born in the middle of the project.

About the author

Blaire Palmer is one of the UK's leading creative thinking partners and executive coaches.

Formerly a BBC journalist, Blaire now specialises in coaching leaders and teams to upgrade their performance and solve problems more creatively. Her clients are major corporations, entrepreneurs and individuals who, like her, strive to be their best and achieve success in whatever area of work or life is most meaningful to them.

Blaire's first book, *The Hyper-Creative Personality*, was published in 2007. She is also a columnist, public speaker and regular guest on BBC Radio 2's Jeremy Vine show.

For more information about Blaire's work, visit her website at www. blairepalmer.com and read her blog at www.letsbesuccessfulagain. com.

Biographies

OLI BARRETT – KEY HOLDER

Social entrepreneur Oli Barrett runs the innovation company Connected Capital and is the founder of Make Your Mark with a Tenner, a national competition in which 10,000 school pupils are given £10 and one month to see what they can achieve.

Oli founded his first company, Amazingyou, at university, growing the team to 150 people in nine cities and hosting events to connect students to young professionals for inspiration and opportunities. After dropping out of university he became a Butlins Redcoat (entertainer and compere) and worked with Hit Entertainment on the launch of the interactive show 'Bob the Builder', before going on to work with the BBC, Disney and Sony Wonder in New York.

Oli brought the concept of Speed Networking to the UK and continues to host events regularly. Other companies he has helped to launch, and in which he remains a shareholder, include SockRush.com (the sock subscription service), Soflow (the business networking site which merged into wis.dm) and FriendsAbroad.com (the world's largest language learning exchange).

CAROLE BLAKE – STAR MAKER

Carole Blake is one of the UK's leading literary agents. She worked in publishing, combining rights selling and contracts, for 14 years before establishing the Carole Blake Literary Agency in 1977 which merged with Julian Friedmann's agency in 1982 to become the Blake Friedmann Literary Agency.

Carole has been President of the Association of Authors' Agents, Chairman of the Society of Bookmen (then only the second woman to hold this position since it was founded in 1921), and Chairman of the book trade charity, the Book Trade Benevolent Society. She is a member of the advisory board for City University's postgraduate publishing course, and the advisory board of the UCL Centre for Publishing, was a judge for the BBC television short story series 'End of Story' in 2004 and has been in *Who's Who* since 1998. In 2005, she recorded her life story as part of the British Library's oral history project, 'Book Trade Lives', the only agent to have been invited to do so.

Carole is the author of *From Pitch to Publication: Everything You Need to Know to Get Your Novel Published* (Macmillan, 1999), now in its tenth printing, and is under contract to write a revised and updated edition. Her clients include Jane Asher, Sheila O'Flanagan, Peter James, Craig Russell, Anne de Courcy and Barbara Erskine.

SHARON CONNOLLY – ENABLER

Sharon Connolly trained as a consultant with Colour Me Beautiful, but quickly developed her own unique style of consultations and is now one of the UK's most successful and sought-after image consultants. She has helped thousands of people to discover how fabulous they can look once they know their rules and gain the confidence to be creative.

Sharon is truly talented at transforming dull, boring wardrobes into combinations of stunning outfits. Her clients are amazed to find they often don't have to buy many new items; they just need a little guidance on how to bring it all to life. A busy mum of two young children, Sharon runs three successful businesses and knows that deciding what to wear might not be at the top of everyone's list each morning, which is why having a wardrobe full of clothes that work – and combine well – is so important.

As well as doing individual consultations, Sharon works with companies to ensure that their employees are portraying the right image. Clients include Microsoft, Unilever, Wyeth Pharmaceuticals, BBC, Channel 4, British Chambers of Commerce, British Heart Foundation, Devere Hotels and UKInbound.

VICKI DAY – ENABLER

Vicki Day specialises in PR and runs Pure Sauce, a consultancy providing advice to the retail industry. She started her retail life on the shop floor after studying manufacturing and retail fashion, then trained as a manager with Jaeger and later became store manager at Lewis's in Manchester. Vicki describes the job as being like running a mini city, full of characters and stories (like when Santa died in his Grotto – he was 75 years old and was buried in his suit. None of the children found out). From there, Vicki went on to work with Ikea, helping the company to plan and build its flagship Croydon store, before moving on to the Leslie Fay company, putting concessions for five American labels in department stores. Later, she worked for a former Lewis's supplier, turning their Zygo label around.

On discovering she had cancer, Vicki took a year off for treatment and relaxation before returning to work for a retail headhunter, only to then retrain as a journalist with London's City University and complete an internship at *Drapers* fashion trade magazine. She draws on her journalism expertise and retail background to help retailers and retail professionals raise their profile in the trade press.

LUCY HARRIS – STAR MAKER

After taking a degree in textile design, Lucy Harris worked as a buyer for Harrods for four years. In 1995 she joined the recruitment world, working first for the retail agency Success Appointments before being approached to establish and run the retail arm of the executive search firm Morgan Chase Group. In 2001, she was approached to join the boutique consultancy Fusion Consulting as a director and, in September 2007, she was appointed retail partner for the global executive search firm The Ashton Partnership.

Over the last two years, Lucy has positioned, amongst others, a chief executive for a luxury children's wear brand; a chief operating officer for a luxury leather brand; a managing director for a TV shopping channel; commercial, product and e-commerce directors at board level for Blacks Leisure Group; a merchandise director at board level for White Stuff; heads of divisions reporting to the European President of TK Maxx; category directors for Disney Consumer Services; a fashion director for John Lewis; and a retail operations director for T-Mobile.

DEBORAH MEREDITH – ENABLER

Deborah Meredith is managing director of City PA, which provides virtual secretarial and business support to executives, small and medium-sized businesses, trades people and public sector clients. The company provides all the support you would expect from a PA, without the headaches of employing a full-time member of staff.

Deborah brings 17 years of experience as an executive PA to the role, working mainly at board level within the construction and finance sectors, although she did venture briefly into advertising, engineering and retail. Deborah's considerable experience and skills enable her to co-ordinate the team at City PA into a highly effective support system for their clients to ensure that they receive the highest quality of service.

JOHN SAVAGE CBE – ENABLER

John Savage is Chief Executive of GWE Business West and has more than 40 years' hands-on business management experience. John spent 16 years in general management in the food production industry and then ran his own international distribution company for five years before joining the Associated Newspaper Group to carry out specialist consultancy work within a number of their subsidiary companies. In 1989, he was appointed Chief Executive of The Bristol Initiative and, from February 1993 became Chief Executive of the Bristol Chamber of Commerce and Initiative, after the merger of these two bodies.

In September 2004, he was appointed Executive Chairman of Business West, the revised joint operating company of the Bristol Chamber and Business Link West, and in April 2008 Chief Executive of its latest iteration – GWE Business West. John is also Vice Chairman of the West of England Partnership, Chairman of the South West Learning and Skills Council and Chairman of the United Bristol Healthcare Trust, as well as holding a number of other board and chairmanship positions in the West Country.

John is dedicated to encouraging partnerships between local government, industry and commerce in order to promote the position of Bristol and its neighbouring communities as a vibrant and vital European city region in the 21st century. He was awarded the CBE for services to Business and Regeneration in the 2006 New Year Honours List.

PHIL TAYLOR – KEY HOLDER

Phil Taylor is Vice President of Human Resources for the International Division of Mattel Inc., the world's leading toy company. He is currently based in the Netherlands and has responsibility for Mattel's human resources (HR) function in 42 sales and marketing businesses outside the USA. Prior to joining Mattel, he held a variety of HR positions with Scottish and Newcastle Breweries plc in the UK.

Phil has worked in many areas of the world, including the UK, Indonesia and Hong Kong (in an Asia Regional capacity) and held European and international HR leadership roles. Much of his career has involved building and developing business leadership teams in both brown field and green field environments for the sales, marketing and manufacturing areas of the business. For a number of years, Phil held a line management role with Mattel in manufacturing, leading teams in production, warehousing and logistics, before continuing with his HR career.

Phil's diverse career, working within a broad variety of countries and cultures, has given him a unique depth and breadth of experience in identifying and developing leaders across the world.

Introduction

What is the recipe for success? What are the secret ingredients? What does it really take to be successful? If you read the auto-biographies of self-made millionaires such as Richard Branson, Duncan Bannatyne and Peter Jones, you'll be told that anyone can do it. Just have a good idea, mix in some belief in yourself and your product, work hard to stir up some interest and some invest-ment and you can make it to the top. If you follow the advice of Jack Welch (former head of the US giant General Electric), add a large spoonful of straight speaking, sieve the mixture rigorously to remove any mediocrity and you too can be the CEO of a multinational company.

Alternatively, open the pages of most self-help books and you'll be told that the recipe is simple: just take a packet of self-confidence and add a pint of passion for what you do, and you'll rise through the ranks to win the top job and the top salary.

Except that there are many people out there basing their success strategy on these step-by-step instructions and finding it isn't working for them. They aren't chief executives or managing directors. They are still languishing in middle management or struggling to get venture capital for their revolutionary invention. These people are passionate about what they do, too. They have the talent and they have the ambition, but they keep being passed over when promotions or other opportunities arise. They have read countless autobiographies and their bookshelves are heaving with self-help books, but the recipe for success still eludes them.

I work as a coach and 'creative thinking partner' for executives and entrepreneurs, helping them to get their head in the right place for ongoing, sustainable success. And I've worked with all kinds of people. Some were destined for greatness or had achieved it already, but others were struggling. And I started to wonder:

> *'What makes the difference between people who effortlessly command respect, admiration and achieve great things and those who plug away, seeming to do all the right stuff but not quite making it?'*

I began to notice that there were some subtle differences between those who had it and those who didn't. And these weren't the differences I had read about in the self-help books or the autobiographies. It was as though there were secret ingredients that no one wanted to talk about, the equivalent of the pinch of saffron or the tablespoon of rosewater that the top chefs add to their restaurant dishes but leave out when they write their cookery books.

THE PROBLEM WITH AUTOBIOGRAPHIES

So, why don't the rich and successful want to share *all* of their secrets with the rest of us?

In part, it is not intentional. Autobiographies will tell you one person's story *from his or her perspective*. And to the individuals concerned, their success seems pre-ordained. As they look back on their humble beginnings, they read meaning into every event and start to believe that something their mother once told them, an early experience of success, or a lesson learnt in their youth led them inexorably to where they are today. They will show you how every twist and turn in their life led them neatly to world domination. Even when things went wrong, it was simply a step along to path to the success they later achieved. They didn't feel disheartened or that their plans had been derailed because they knew it would work out in the end.

Well, of course! They are writing from that end point, with the benefit of hindsight and from the comfort of their luxury home in the Bahamas. From there, it is easy to imagine that their success was always meant to be. And reading books like this can lead anyone to believe that just when things seem to be at their bleakest, there is always a miracle waiting around the corner.

Except that for most people, there *is* no miracle. They work and struggle and pursue their dream, but miracles don't happen. Reverse-engineering the success of someone like Richard Branson won't give you a step-by-step guide to your own success. It simply shows how events turned out for one man. Add to this the fact that successful people may not be the best judge of why they've ended up where they are. After all, they only have their own experience to go by. They have no basis for comparison.

Successful people don't always know what they are doing which is so different to everyone else. Reading interviews with successful people often tells you nothing you didn't already know. Rachel Bridge, author of *How I Made It* says that passion is a key ingredient for the entrepreneurs she interviewed:

> Ask Harry Cragoe [founder of PJ Smoothies] to tell you about his smoothies and he will happily talk about them for hours. The same passion for their business applies to everyone else in the book. If you do not believe 100 per cent in what you are doing, you will never be able to persuade anyone else – investors, customers, bank managers, partners or employees – to believe in it either.[1]

However, many unsuccessful people have passion too. They work night and day on their invention, their craft or their skill and talk about little else. And yet it's still not enough. But when successful people say it was their 'passion' that set them apart, we all take note.

In short, then, successful people are not the best analysts of what makes them different. They are just doing what comes instinctively, just being themselves, and they can't understand why the results aren't the same for others when they follow the same recipe. Most successful people don't spend a large amount of time inspecting their own navel. They are too busy getting on with the job in hand to look objectively at their motivations, their values or their personal qualities. When asked why they believe they have made it, they often shrug and try, helpfully, to offer an explanation such as 'determination'. It is a stab in the dark.

It may also be that successful people do not *want* to tell us the whole truth. After all, this secret ingredient is what gives them an edge so even if they know what it is, they might not want the whole world to know. It just makes business sense to keep a few secrets from your potential competition. Equally, the secret ingredients might not be very attractive. Some might not want to admit that they got their first step on the ladder by misleading a friend, selling goods on the black market or by lying on their CV.

THE PROBLEM WITH SELF-HELP BOOKS

So powerful are the clichés about success that they are rarely questioned rigorously. The authors of self-help books often interview the 'usual suspects' in order to gain an insight in to the secret recipe for success. In this case, readers will get more than one person's word for it in the form of a selection of quotes from our most well-known and well respected business leaders. They are asked what makes them successful and, as explained above, they try to be helpful and offer an explanation. This explanation is then taken as gospel by the author and repeated to readers who are left to wonder why it isn't working for them. But because these pearls of wisdom come from the horse's mouth, it is taken as fact. It must be true because Gordon Ramsay said it and look how successful he is!

Let's take some examples such as the oft-repeated maxim 'dress for success'. Any self-help book focused on career success will tell you that you need to dress the part if you want the job and their interviewees will back this up. It's true that some of my best clients have been immaculately dressed. They were suited and booted straight out of the pages of 'Executives R Us'. But some were, frankly, a mess and no strangers to ripped jeans and unkempt hair. And some extremely smartly dressed individuals don't make it beyond the first line of management, so clearly clothes do not tell the whole story. Of course, industry norms play a part. In the media industry, for example, denim is far more acceptable than it is in the world of high finance. But I began to wonder whether 'dressing for success' really made a fundamental difference. Your image may be a part of your success but the issue is far more complex than simply kitting yourself out in the right gear.

And let's look at emotional intelligence. As an Executive Coach I am well versed in the concept that it is 'EQ' which distinguishes exceptional leaders from average leaders, and largely I agree. This theory claims that without empathy skills, highly tuned self-awareness and the ability to work as a member of a team, one cannot achieve real success.

Yet when I looked at some of my most successful clients, that wasn't always what I found. Most were part of a team and they realised that no-one makes it alone. But they were also the boss and they made the final decision, often based on what looked and sounded like a lot like gut instinct, rather than empathy.

In terms of self-awareness, many would not – or could not – explain their deepest motivations, the reasons they wanted to hit certain goals or why they had achieved great success. Nor were they interested in such self-examination. Anything that sounded too much like 'coaching' was a total turn-off and any self-development work had to be disguised as something else. And while many were excellent judges of people, they were often loathed by some as much as they were loved by others. They had the hide of a rhino and had decided many years ago that their job was to do the right thing rather than to make friends.

Sensing that taking the word of a small selection of high profile successful people or self-help gurus was not going to give me any fresh insights, I turned my attention to a much-ignored class of people who actually have the power to make and break individuals trying to get to the top. I believe the experts on success and the holders of the 'secret recipe' are a group of hugely powerful but often overlooked individuals without whom no one makes it into the boardroom. I call them Enablers, Star Makers and Key Holders.

ENABLERS, STAR MAKERS AND KEY HOLDERS

You can't be successful without them. No-one started up their dream business without a family loan, a friendly bank manager or venture capital. No-one made it in the corporate world without a headhunter, a nod from someone in Human Resources or a passionate internal advocate. No-one wowed their audience without an agent, a coach or a stylist.

If you want to be successful, in whatever field that might be and however you want to define it, you'll need a team of backroom champions to make it happen. It is these Star Makers who mould you in to someone worthy of the boardroom. It is these Key Holders who open doors for you. And it is these Enablers who know what it takes. . . and whether you've got it.

Ever wonder why you didn't get that promotion? Ever see some contemporary of yours on TV talking about her new book/play/number one single and wonder 'Why isn't that me?' Ever wonder, while you stare at a blank order book, why someone else is making a fortune and you're not?

Well, it is possible, just possible, that those people really do have something that you don't have. Yet. And the people who can tell you what that 'something' is are right here in this book.

WHAT GIVES STAR MAKERS, KEY HOLDERS AND ENABLERS BETTER INSIGHT?

Firstly, they see both the hopeful and the hopeless. For example, a top literary agent may receive 200 unsolicited manuscripts a week but will only select 10 new clients a year to represent. Most people who write to her do not make the grade. The agent will know what she's looking for and what just won't work. Her insight will help you get it right.

Secondly, they have nothing to hide. In fact, they have a vested interest in telling you the truth. Venture capitalists don't want to waste their time. If they can articulate why most people who approach them are rejected, they may be able to put off a few people who lack the talent (or whatever else it is that makes the difference) and so receive pitches that are of a more appropriate quality.

Thirdly, these are the kinds of people you need on your side if you are going to make a splash professionally. It almost doesn't matter whether they are right or wrong. It's what they think that matters. Without the support, contacts and advice of these people you're just an ambitious person with nothing to show for it.

THE STAR MAKERS

In some walks of life, you can't get far without Star Makers. These will include an agent if you want to do anything creative, a sponsor or venture capitalist if you want to set up in business or a headhunter if you want to make it in the corporate world.

These individuals are basically talent-spotters. They may have been watching you for some time before they are in a position to help you or before you are ready for their help. For example, you may have visited a venture capitalist before with an idea but it wasn't quite the right one at the right time. Two years later, the timing might be right and the idea is a winner. I have some personal experience of this. I sent off many ideas for books to agents and publishers before hitting upon one which attracted attention.[2] Once I had an agent the way became easier, and doors that were previously shut opened a crack.

Star Makers recognise talent quickly. They need to see past the inexperience, the bravado, or the youth of the person before them and see a gift that can be honed, polished or set on the right path with their help. As Star Maker and headhunter Lucy Harris says:

> You can summarise someone in the first three seconds but it is not always accurate. If you see confidence or even arrogance you can't necessarily understand it immediately. It could be down to nerves.

To attract the attention of a Star Maker, you will also need to be what they are looking for at the time they are looking for it. Whatever your field, business is business, and according to Carole Blake, a top literary agent who represents best-selling authors like Craig Russell and Peter James, life isn't always fair:

> You see a lot of unpublished authors bemoaning the fact that a published author is good looking with blue eyes. The publishing industry isn't daft – it helps to look good – but you won't be published without talent. Having said that, if all else is equal and I have a choice of three novels but one of the authors is funny, or in her 70s or 17 years old, that does help. It is hard to stand out if you are writing your first novel in your 40s.

Confidence is also an attractive quality, one which helps you deal with rejection, according to Blake:

> The people I represent sometimes need boosting rather than being arrogant. You do need to be fairly self-confident to be a

writer but many authors, because they get so many rejections, can become bitter and that's not pleasant because it doesn't help them. Sometimes I have rejected authors and got furious diatribes back and I think they might be in the wrong business if they can't learn how to accept rejection graciously. I don't know any published authors who haven't also been rejected at some time.

THE KEY HOLDERS

Key Holders are influential people who will open doors for you. They don't always want responsibility for 'making' you, but they may be fans of yours, 'centres of influence' who enjoy giving other people a leg up as they were given a leg up in the past.

Phil Taylor, Vice President of International Human Resources for toy maker Mattel, is just one of those. He'll give a helping hand to someone he thinks has the right stuff:

A lot of what I am doing is seeing what talent we've got, where they are at, what they are doing, what we need to do, how we develop them. Whenever I go to other countries, I always take time to meet the people they see as 'high potentials' in that country so I can get more involved in their long term development.

Key Holders tend to be well-respected and plugged into good networks. They know everyone and everyone knows them. And they seem to have a genuine desire to connect people up. Oli Barrett is a networker who has shares in a variety of business he has helped to start up:

I don't believe someone should have to struggle for months to make the right connection when I know the person they should meet. What holds people back more than anything is that they haven't met the right person. I want to help people I believe in, I want to help save them time. It is massively rewarding spending time with high energy, highly creative, dynamic people who make things happen and seeing their often swift progress.

Consequently, everyone wants a piece of them. Getting to be in their inner circle is a big step towards accessing their network. But they guard their space passionately. Oli Barrett does this by managing his huge network very carefully:

> I might have 650 friends on Facebook but I have 10 close friends. Time with them is absolutely sacred. I don't do business with any of my friends. In terms of people I do business with, no more than a dozen are in the friends category but even then I am quite careful about the time I spend with them. I have also found having a simple personal website with a 'Contact us' form rather than an e-mail address is fantastic because it is attached to an explanation of what I do so approaches tend to be more relevant. Otherwise you are just someone who knows everyone and everyone wants to know someone like that don't they? I try to be careful about saying 'Yes' to face time with someone when a 10 minute phone call is as effective. And I host events on a monthly basis where I have 100 people in a room at the same time and offer something to them which might be valuable to them – the chance to meet other people. I 'cast' every one of these so it is an interesting blend of people and this is a way that I can connect with them even if it is just through the invitation.

THE ENABLERS

The third category of behind-the-scenes powerhouses is the Enablers. These are your secret weapon, trusted advisers, honest friends who tell it to you like it is and make up for the gaps in your own personality or skill set.

Enablers include internal sponsors or mentors who may receive nothing but a sense of satisfaction out of helping you. But is their motivation always so altruistic?

John Savage's motivation is selfish in some ways. He wants to work with people who share his values and work well with him so he mentors those in his sphere. However, as Chief Executive of Business West and Chairman of the United Bristol Healthcare Trust, he is also motivated out of a deeper, more spiritual belief:

> Homo sapiens are the epitome of the Creation. I am not a God-pusher but I am a believer. And I believe we have a duty to make the world work as well as we can. If you sit back and think everything will turn out alright, it won't. You have to shape things and people.

Vicki Day, who provides PR services for top-flight executives, says that behind every successful person is a partner – either in business or at home – who makes things happen. Without this partner, even the most successful people lack the skills to achieve anything on their own:

> Successful people of that level have a kind of OCD. My best friend is hugely successful, recently selling his business for £45m. He has no interpersonal skills. He is void of personality. But he has teamed up with someone else who has. When someone is successful there's often a ying and yang thing going on. Together they are a winning team.

As an executive coach, I have been the Enabler for successful people. Some meet me when they are in their prime; they are confident and focused and use their time with me as a sounding board. Self-doubt and self-analysis are not a part of our work together. Instead, we brainstorm ideas and bounce concepts around until the client has total clarity. Some clients, however, do suffer greatly from a lack of confidence. They use their coaching sessions to 'get in the zone' before an important meeting, presentation or confrontation. To the outside world they are self-assured and never lose their way, but it is the Enablers who see the messy 'insides' that lie at the heart of many a successful person. Trust, then, is vital. The whole image will be shot to pieces if the truth about the successful person were to come out in public.

Sometimes you find an Enabler on purpose. Many top executives have turned to Sharon Connolly, an image consultant who works with senior business people one-to-one or through workshops, as well as helping people taking a career break and even the odd TV presenter and actor. When people seek her out, they are often at a crunch point in their lives, either professionally or personally.

A lot of the time they are at a life change. They have reached 30, 40, 50, got divorced, got a promotion, something that has triggered them looking in the mirror and saying 'I don't like what I see'. They aren't car-crash bad. They just lack the confidence to know what to do about it. I enable them to take control of their own image so they are aware of the impact of their decisions. If they want to dye their hair blue and wear red socks that's fine, but I make them aware that in certain areas that is going to alienate people and in others it is going to open doors for them.

But some Enablers are found by happy accident: they're childhood friends, college roommates, or a wife who has a particular skill at making her husband look great (or vice versa).

In this book we will be hearing from a selection of Star Makers, Key Holders and Enablers. Not all of them will agree that my final list of ingredients is definitive. As you'll see in Chapter 11, many felt that other ingredients were vital to the mix. But the selection here are ingredients that most of our experts agreed were important, elements that they saw regularly in their favourite clients, colleagues and stars.

And all are successful in their own right. They have made their way to the top and can share some of the lessons they learnt along the way. Of course, their perspective will be subjective, but put together with their observations about people they have helped to stardom and those they have rejected, it makes for a pretty rich, rounded and powerful recipe.

Your job is to ask yourself honestly whether these are qualities you either want to replicate or are capable of replicating ... or whether it is a case of 'You've either got it or you haven't'.

REFERENCES

1 Bridge, Rachel. *How I Made It*. p.11. London: Kogan Page, 2005.
2 Palmer, Blaire. *The Hyper-Creative Personality*. London: New Holland, 2007.

Ingredient 1

Manners

To anyone watching the popular TV programmes *The Apprentice*, *The F Word* or *Dragons' Den*, it would appear that rudeness is the 'quality' that will guarantee you a fast track to success. Being the king of the put-down or the queen of cruelty has become almost a cliché. I remember attending an audition at a TV production company which was looking for a coach to take part in a new reality show. I didn't get the part. The reason? I wasn't rude enough.

But what plays well on television doesn't work so well in the boardroom. One ingredient that was mentioned by almost all of the Star Makers, Key Holders and Enablers I interviewed for this book was good old-fashioned manners. Rudeness in the workplace is widespread. Recent research from Australia and New Zealand showed that one in five people had experienced bad manners at work at least once in the previous month,[1] while in the UK, 68 per cent of participants in a survey by Canon said they had been spoken to rudely at work, leading to what the research called 'office rage'.[2] And in a survey by NFI Research, a division of the Net Future Institute, only about a third of senior executives and managers could say that their people always practised good manners.[3]

Technology has been blamed for the increase in rudeness at work. It is easier to be tough or terse in an e-mail than face to face – people often miss out 'please' and 'thank you' because electronic communication is perceived as less formal. However, as e-mails can't convey tone of voice, they can be easily misinterpreted.

Once, in a team I was working with, I observed two colleagues exchanging e-mails over a period of about 10 minutes. They sat on either side of a glass partition and I watched, incredulous, as e-mails flew back and forth and the authors' faces became more frustrated, angry and aggressive. In the end, one could stand it no longer. She stood up and stormed in to the other's cubicle. It became clear within seconds that there had been a misunderstanding and, in fact, both women agreed completely about the course of action needed.

There is a hangover effect from such encounters. Although the misunderstanding was identified in this case, no one can erase the 10-minute 'office rage' that occurred or who was responsible. We can forgive, but it is harder to forget and in this way we build up animosity towards colleagues based on absolutely nothing. Such animosity is bad for business. In the above-mentioned Australian and New Zealand research, it was shown that incivility had a detrimental impact on performance at work. The survey found that organisations with a high incidence of incivility had a high percentage of poor and inconsistent performers and this, of course, has an impact on results.

There is a belief that, in order to be successful in a business, you need a large helping of brusqueness. A 'survival of the fittest' culture has evolved where people are expected to cope with the pressures of the office and accept that rudeness or lack of common courtesy is part of modern life. 'If you can't take the heat, get out of the kitchen' is a clichéd response to anyone who complains that the culture is impolite.

However, many of those who have made it to the very top do not seem to have followed this recipe. They recognise that people still respond most favourably to good old-fashioned manners and they go above and beyond their duty to demonstrate this. John

Savage CBE, Chief Executive of Business West, typifies these traditional values and expects to see them in those he mentors. An Enabler who is passionate about helping people develop their potential, he believes manners are tied up with a genuine compassion for others. Self-centredness, by contrast, is a dead end for achieving big things. He says:

> Ruthlessness and crassness concern me. I ask, 'Do you have a capacity for compassion? Can you see a child fall over in the playground and feel the pain in your own knee?' After all, what is success all about? Being happy and getting satisfaction. If you own seven cars and three houses, what's that doing for you? The cult of selfishness was absolutely pushed by Thatcher. This is patently wrong.

Deborah Meredith has a lifetime of experience as a PA to chief executives and chairmen. As an Enabler, she wields huge power. Without the approval of someone like her, no one gets to see the boss. And good manners give some people the edge:

> One of the best examples I remember from when I was a PA was a company who sent a direct mail piece saying they would telephone in two days. When their salesman called, he asked for half an hour with the boss, I said no. He called again and I said no. This went on for three or four weeks. Then he asked, 'What do I have to do to get a meeting with him?', so I said I was quite partial to white lilies. A bouquet was delivered. Then more came later. Just for the sheer cheek, I said he could have a half-hour meeting. Subsequently he got the contract. I wouldn't always recommend this, but be upfront with the gatekeeper, have a conversation with the PA, maybe even a meeting with the PA. Cheek and persistence sometimes work.

IT'S IN THE NAME

So what form can good manners take? Addressing people correctly is a good start. Getting their name right and remembering it the next time you meet them sounds simple, but it is effective because so many people can't seem to master the skill.

Memory expert David Thomas suggests that you create an image when you hear someone's name for the first time. Make sure you have heard the name correctly, even if that means asking again, and then make an association. If someone is called Julie, you might think of jewellery as it sounds similar. Look at the person and take in some of his or her more obvious characteristics. Imagine Julie wearing a mass of jewels, picturing the way they glint in the light and the sound they might make. Make the image as vivid as you can so that the next time you see Julie, you will immediately remember the association and her name will come to mind.

It is also good manners to tell people your name in a way they can remember. I always make a memorable association for the person I am meeting by saying, 'Blaire, like the former Prime Minister'. Alternatively, you can repeat your name a couple of times in conversation. And you can help others when they are introducing you to people. After they have introduced you, repeat your name as you shake the new person's hand. If you sense someone struggling to remember your name as they attempt to introduce you, don't hesitate to introduce yourself, thereby getting them out of a tricky situation and giving you a chance to enunciate your name properly for the new person you are meeting.

True business etiquette dictates that introductions are determined by precedence. The person who holds the position of highest authority in an organisation takes precedence over others who work there. For example, you have to introduce your company's chief executive to a colleague. The basic rule is that the name of the person of greater authority is always spoken first: 'Ms Senior, I would like to introduce Mr Junior.'

A handwritten note has become a powerful statement of good manners and consideration since the dominance of e-mail and type-written communication. Star Maker Carole Blake is one of the top literary fiction agents in the UK, representing best-selling authors such as Peter James and Craig Russell. When deciding who to represent, manners is a vital consideration:

> Peter James is one of my best-selling authors. He is very polite, courteous, he remembers people's names and people will go that extra mile for him. Maeve Binchy [not one of Carole's clients] writes thank-you postcards to people in shops that have invited her to do a reading. When it comes to individual people's efforts, you want your assistant to recommend to friends that they read someone's book because they were so polite when they came into the office. I want to make sure that authors don't turn into brats. I work all the time – I don't have weekends – so I want people who inhabit my life to be people I can admire.

It is much easier these days to find out the name of the person you want to speak or write to without resorting to techniques worthy of a private detective. A quick Internet search will tell you who to speak to and how to spell their name. Despite this, I regularly get e-mails to 'Blair' or even 'Mr Blair' and Carole Blake, co-founder of literary agency Blake Friedmann, says that her business partner Julian Friedmann regularly gets letters starting 'Dear Blake'.

SHOW SOME RESPECT

The clothes we wear also demonstrate our manners. Enabler Sharon Connolly, an image consultant for senior executives, believes that dressing appropriately is a sign of respect for others:

> When you go for interview, by wearing a suit and cleaning your

shoes and showing up on time you are demonstrating respect. But this idea of 'Sunday Best' is something we have lost both in society in general and in the workplace because of the culture of casual dress. And I think leaders should show the way by dressing a little bit smarter than everyone else. It doesn't matter if you aren't customer-facing. Your colleagues – your boss and your peer group – are your customers too. They are responsible in some way for giving you access to the next rung on the ladder. A smart, successful person works their internal network as well as their external network. And the clothes you wear are part of that.

In order to achieve great success, you need the expertise and assistance of people like Carole Blake or John Savage. They have to want to help you, spend time developing you and see their investment pay off. Good manners seem to buy a lot of credit and goodwill.

In his book *The Seven Habits of Highly Effective People*, Stephen Covey uses the analogy of the bank account to explain how we build and withdraw credit from people around us. He explains:[4]

If I make deposits in an Emotional Bank Account with you through courtesy, kindness, honesty and keeping my commitments to you, I build up a reserve . . . But if I have a habit of showing discourtesy, disrespect . . . eventually my Emotional Bank Account is overdrawn. The trust level gets very low.

Once you are 'in the red' in the Emotional Bank Account, any withdrawal, even accidental, puts you further in debt. If you are late for an appointment, make a poor presentation, slip up on a piece of work, come into conflict with a colleague or even take genuine sick leave there is little capacity for generosity in the people around you if you have already put yourself in the red because of previous disrespectful behaviour.

It might seem unfair that you have been judged so harshly for something outside of your control. You may even observe other people making a similar mistake and being treated with more consideration. But ask yourself whether you have built up enough 'credit' through good manners with colleagues to endure difficult times. People will be forgiving if you are in credit with them. However, they will come down hard – maybe even blocking your opportunity to progress in the organisation – if you are continually in debt.

This is not to say that successful people always keep their cool, but that they have earned enough credit to keep your support even when they let off steam. Enabler Vicki Day has seen many outbursts in her years in retail:

> Philip Green can melt earwax when he goes on the verbal offensive, but if you stand up to him he'll get it off his chest and then it's over and done with. Because you understand that, you don't want to make the same mistake twice. But if you've got someone who is always chewing your head off, you tend to make more mistakes.

Of course, many of us are motivated to behave rudely as a result of the constant rudeness of others. Even the most placid of us can become enraged and act out of character when we are put under extreme pressure. However, imagine your conversations are like a movie script. You can't write the other players' lines, but you can write your own and, when you change your script, other people have to change theirs. If you react as they do, they'll continue to be rude, but if you respond with grace, patience and good manners, they may follow suit. In addition, by following their lead, you lose the higher moral ground. If the conflict does escalate and comes to the attention of a more senior authority, you will have more support if you behaved impeccably.

If there is a problem with a colleague, discuss it with him or her face to face, explaining specifically what offended you and suggesting ways to work more effectively together in future. As difficult as it may be, use a neutral tone of voice otherwise your words may be polite, but your tone can betray any frustration or aggression you may be feeling. A quiet word like this may resolve the problem or may be a formality before taking the issue further. But remember: don't do it by e-mail! As we have already seen, e-mails can be the *cause* of misunderstanding and poor communication and should not be relied upon for something as subtle as giving feedback to a colleague.

You always have the option to use your company's formal complaints procedure. However, you may decide this is not advantageous or necessary. It may be seen as an extreme reaction to a minor conflict which could be resolved informally. In addition, their rudeness may not be inhibiting your route to success and, in fact, may work in your favour by setting you apart as someone who understands acceptable standards of behaviour and lives by an admirable moral code. And this is one of the ingredients that is recognised in most organisations. Mattel's Phil Taylor is a Key Holder within the organisation and has a responsibility for opening doors to talented individuals in the business. He believes that cut-throat behaviour should not be rewarded:

> You want to see people who are passionate, you want to see people who care, who work hard to get their mission across. They don't need to be rude or aggressive to others to do that. I don't think it is our culture. I don't think it drives a healthy organisation.

It may be surprising that in today's fast-paced business world, manners are still such an important ingredient in the mix. But it is worth mentioning that not one of the experts interviewed for this book felt that good manners were optional. Although many had seen rude-ness in senior people, they would not willingly assist, promote, enable or work alongside anyone who constantly exhibited such behaviour beyond doing the very minimum which was required. Given that a leg-up or a good word are so important in a competitive environment, it is as well to have as many fans as possible rooting for you.

MANNERS RECIPE

- Remember people's names, no matter how junior they are. Remember personal aspects such as the names of their children or what work their partner does.
- Introduce people to one another, the most senior first.
- Remember please and thank you. Handwritten notes are often appreciated.
- Dress smartly, even if you never see customers.
- Keep your cool whenever possible. You can only afford to 'melt earwax' if you have built up credit in the Emotional Bank Account. However, this doesn't mean you can't also be tough where needed.
- Listen properly and always look people in the eye, smiling where appropriate. Show that you appreciate people.
- Remember that good manners are good for business.

REFERENCES

1 www.humanresourcesmagazine.com.au/articles/F7/0c04e6f7.asp?Type=59&Category=917
2 www.binfo.co.uk/2008/01/18/bad-manners-tips-uk-workers-over-the-edge
3 www.cio.com/article/141452/Too_Few_Manners_at_Work
4 Covey, Stephen R. *The Seven Habits of Highly Effective People*. p.188. London: Simon & Schuster UK Ltd, 1989.

Ingredient 2

Focus

Saying 'please' and 'thank you' will make you easier to work with, but 'focus' is the necessary ingredient for getting things done.

Focus comes in many forms. It is the ingredient which fuels the successful person's drive to succeed. They want to see results and, no matter how many times they fail, they get back on the path again and resume their journey, never losing their focus on the end goal. It's also the ingredient which enables them to get things done despite opposition. Many successful leaders and entrepreneurs have faced criticism or even rejection along the way to success, but they kept pressing on, convinced that someone, somewhere would eventually back them and their idea.

And focus is the ingredient that provides the momentum which other people can get behind. The successful person has his or her eyes front, looking towards the horizon and guiding everyone else towards that same distant point. While other people may occasionally lose that sense of perspective, often referred to as the big picture or the vision, the successful person always has it in their sights.

Focus is about knowing where to look, be that the overall objective, the big picture or the job in hand in order to turn a venture into a success; it is about knowing what is important and not caving in to distractions. When a business fails, it is often because no one was focused on the priorities, so firefighting took over and direction was lost. People who head up successful businesses do not allow this to happen.

Focus is not actually a single ingredient but more a mix of spices – a 'garamasala' if you like. Get the balance wrong and your mixture will be too sour, too spicy or simply too bland. However, stubbornness, self-confidence, persistence, and maybe even arrogance, can all be part of the blend.

Personal PR expert Vicki Day says that successful people often appear to wear blinkers, so great is their focus on the goal:

> They have massive inner belief and the ability not to listen to detractors. Some people are put off by what other people will say, but they don't care what you think. Maybe they are cocky, arrogant, self-confident. They have to have these qualities in order to think 'I am going to succeed no matter what'. They have to pitch their idea to five people who tell them it is rubbish and then ring another five people. They have an inner drive.

WHAT TO FOCUS ON

So, what are successful people focusing on? According to research by Professor Graham Jones and Olympic swimmer, Adrian Moorhouse,[1] successful performers report that focusing on the following is hugely important:

1. **What is controllable** While many of us spend a lot of our time worrying about what lies outside our control, those at the top of their game identify the factors that are outside their influence and then focus on what they can control. You cannot control someone else's performance, e.g. how a competitor will do in a particular race, but you can control how you perform.
2. **Getting the process right** Exceptional performers have a big goal (e.g. to win the 2012 Olympic Gold), but they don't focus on that daily as they train. Instead they focus on excellence in

every step, stroke or throw. It is the same in any field – business, the arts, academia – get the process right and the outcomes take care of themselves.

3. **Stay in the moment** While it is important to learn from the past, living in the past is not helpful. Equally, always living in the future is a distraction. As Jones and Moorhouse put it: 'Some golfers who find themselves five-under-par after seven holes get carried away by thoughts of a very low score. That's almost as bad as being five-over and thinking they are going to score in the 80s, rather than focusing on what they have to do right here and how.'[2]

4. **Focus on the positives** Thinking about your worst-case scenario is a ticket to failure. Taunting yourself with 'What if this happens?' is likely to bring about exactly the outcome you dread the most. Instead, peak performance requires a focus on what you are good at and what has gone well in the past.

5. **Keep a cool head** Focusing on remaining calm when the adrenaline is pumping means that you can control the jitters that plague many performers. It is vital to be passionate, but it is important that passion doesn't overwhelm you when it counts.

As we can see, those at the top make choices about what to focus on. Sometimes they will be looking inside themselves; at other times they will be looking into the distance. They have incredible control over their mindset, which means they do not get nudged off their course easily by something as inconvenient as a rejection letter, a poor result or a bout of insecurity.

FOCUS VS STUBBORNESS

Of course, that doesn't mean successful people are cut off from reality. They take note of failure or setbacks but only as an opportunity to learn, not as a trigger to lose faith in themselves and their ability to achieve a goal.

Dragons' Den tycoon Peter Jones believes the two qualities that all successful entrepreneurs have are determination and perseverance. For him, perseverance is what helps him to overcome obstacles. Preferring to talk about 'feedback' than failure, he says the tycoon's mindset is always to see every business venture 'failure' as an opportunity for feedback and education in order to avoid making the same mistake again. His focus, or persistence, means that he does not allow failure to affect his state of mind. He doesn't allow himself to read a deeper message into these failures such as 'Maybe I am no good at this'. Instead he picks himself up and starts again:

> When I start a new business or invest in one, there is one trait that is always present – a determination to win and be successful . . . Obstacles are there to be overcome.[3]

Focus is not simply stubbornness. Knowing how long to persist with an idea is vital for success. Many wannabe successes think they are being focused when they stick with a no-hoper idea for too long, sinking their life savings in to it and sacrificing everything they have when the more astute business person would have called it a day and moved on. Their focus is in the wrong place. They are so fearful of failure that they cannot read the writing on the wall. They are focused on proving something, being right or making a quick buck, rather than on long-term sustainable success. They don't want to raise their head to see the truth, that their venture is dead.

I worked with a client many years ago who wanted to win a 'boss of the year' award and showered his small (but rapidly growing) staff with added extras – gym membership, bonuses, healthcare insurance, even the use of a lifestyle manager. He measured the success of his business by how many people he employed and how much they loved him. His focus was on himself and his popularity, even though if you had asked him he would have said his focus was on the well-being of his staff. In fact, his focus should have been on sustainable bottom line growth. That would have been the way to ensure all his people had a job for life. Very soon, though, he had to make redundancies. No need to ask how popular he was then.

On the other hand, many of us are also prone to believing the naysayers and giving up too soon. Perhaps the opportunity to make millions was just around the corner, if only we had the conviction to hang in there. In this case our focus is on cynics, critics and risk-avoiders. We care too much what other people say and lose sight of our instincts and of the evidence. We are distracted by the voices in our head and the voices in our immediate vicinity. The trick, of course, is knowing when to listen to the feedback you receive and when to block out the noise.

Many successful people have experienced failure during their professional lives. Just as Peter Jones describes, they did not take it personally, but used the knowledge they gained to keep going with their overall mission. As he points out, as well as the ability to stay on track, flexibility must always go into the 'garamasala'; the ability to adapt to changing circumstance and even drop the project you are working on if it no longer looks like it will succeed. That doesn't mean you have lost focus, only that you have focused on what is important rather than fixating on one particular means to get there.

It is the effective combination of perseverance and the ability to change tack or even stop what you are doing altogether that is so unusual and which separates those who achieve huge success from those who don't.

Businessman Chris Gorman followed up his success with his mobile phone retail company DX Communications by investing £500,000 in setting up a recording studio. When he lost it all a year later, he was not discouraged:

It was a great learning experience for me to feel the pain of failure because it taught me that I should stick with things I know and understand. It was better it happened then than when I had £20 million to lose.[4]

What these people are able to do is analyse failure and draw out the lesson. Interpret your mistake incorrectly and you will continue to make it; address it effectively and your next venture will be more successful. Of course, this doesn't mean that successful people set out to fail. They aim for success – that's where their focus is. But in order to break new ground, take advantage of a new opportunity or improve their performance on previous years, they must take risks. And when we take risks, there is always a chance of failure.

Successful people experience frustration, even anger, like everyone else when this happens. But they know how to handle it, says Executive PA and Enabler Deborah Meredith:

They may have a bad day, or even a bad week, but they pull themselves out of it. We all have our moments, but they have more than their fair share. They get it out of their system by letting off steam, and then they are back asking, 'What did we learn?' They have a rant – you might think World War Three is about to start – and then we are best friends again. But that's important. Those who let it fester are awful and it isn't nice working for them. It's better to slam a few doors, disappear for a bit, then come back and it's all blown over. It is like opening the windows to let bad air out.

Deborah has worked for chief executive officers (CEOs) and chairmen and chairwomen throughout her career. She has seen them behind closed doors when they are struggling to get the balance right between driving forward or moving on to something new:

> They are certainly stubborn, but not so stubborn that they
> would cut off their nose to spite their face. They fight their
> corner, but when it is pointed out that things could be done a
> different way, they do consider it. They are strong-willed,
> determined, but always ready to listen to different points of
> view. That said, they make sure their opinion is heard. They are
> stubborn in that way.

Most top executives have not landed their job without the help of a
headhunter. Top jobs tend to go to people who are known in their
industry and come with a hefty recommendation. An executive
search professional will connect the company in need with a perfect-
fit candidate. Lucy Harris is a Star Maker who works as a headhunter,
specialising in the retail sector. She can quickly tell the difference
between someone who has the qualities to succeed and someone
who does not. Getting the right balance between stubbornness and
flexibility is fundamental, but is complicated further by the needs of
the changing market:

> You need focus and drive. Do you need to be stubborn to
> maintain that focus and continue to get there? Potentially. You
> stick with Plan A; you don't keep looking at Plan C. However,
> I can contradict that straight away by saying you need to be
> very flexible. In this market, if you are exceptionally stubborn
> and believed to be averse to change and inflexible, that's a
> bad thing.

PERIPHERAL VISION
One of the problems in possessing a great degree of focus is that you
may miss out on ideas and information which lie in your peripheral
vision. The most successful people have learnt to rely on others to
bring them information which may lie outside their precise focus, but
which is still relevant to the success of the company.

This might include developments in other industries which don't directly impact yours but may, in future, affect the environment in which you operate. How will changes in the Internet world (such as social networking sites) affect the expectations of your staff? How will oil prices affect your ability to buy certain products? How will advances in medicine or our understanding of climate change affect the world order in 10 or 20 years? None of us is insulated from events elsewhere in the world. One only has to look at the impact on the whole world economy of the 2008 credit crunch in the United States to see how a butterfly effect can occur and how links between seemingly unrelated parts of our society begin to emerge. While you are focusing on your business or your project, the world is turning.

Expecting one individual to have both focus and peripheral vision, to be looking around a subject as well as directly at it, is expecting too much. In my experience, this is one of the key factors which holds leaders back, keeping them in middle management rather than progressing further up their organisation. The desire to do it all alone has brought down many potential high flyers and is an obstacle to success. If you want to make it big, acknowledge that you can't do it all alone. Focus on whatever is important to you but recognise you can't focus on everything at once.

HOW TO FOCUS

Where does this sense of focus come from? Why are some people able to keep the bigger picture in their minds at all times, when the rest lose their sense of purpose and get lost in the everyday details?

A focus must resonate with you. It doesn't matter whether you are motivated by money, by the desire to make the world a better place or by a belief in the products your company produces, whatever your focus, it needs to be a natural fit for you. If your company makes widgets and you are expected to get excited about being the biggest widget manufacturer in the world without actually caring for the product or for world domination, you are likely to lose your focus quickly.

The product or service that your company provides may not even be your chief focus. Instead, you might believe your mission is to help people in your organisation to achieve their full potential, or maybe your focus is on your personal success – getting to the top of the company or making as much money as you can. As long as you get the opportunity to promote and maintain this focus, and as long as your focus is connected with what makes the business successful, you can achieve great results.

This is why focus can look like selfishness, according to Key Holder Phil Taylor. Successful people are successful because they have seized opportunities to do something they are personally passionate about:

> They only do the things that drive their ambition, so it can look selfish. But they retain their focus. They don't get distracted by peripherals. They focus on the big things that make the big difference.

In the end, your focus chooses *you* rather than you choosing it. Everyone has innate motivations. Discovering yours and then designing your life and work around it is the simplest way to stay focused. You do not need to be reminded of your focus because it is part of who you are.

Think about times when you have been completely absorbed in what you were doing, when you woke up in the morning desperate to pick up where you left off. Perhaps you were more like this in your childhood than in recent years? Maybe there was a project you worked on early in your career which lit your fire, or a place where the work itself was mundane but the people made it worthwhile. What was it about this experience that drove you? If you have more than one experience like this, what do they have in common? This is how you begin to discover your natural focus.

This 'natural fit' requirement is why some people excel in certain environments, but cannot make a success of others. One of my clients, who we will call Steve, excels in turning around struggling businesses. Steve likes to be parachuted in to a business when there is a real possibility the company may have to shut down. He has no trouble keeping his focus in a life-and-death situation, but when the turnaround is successful and jobs in the company are safe, Steve's mind begins to wander. He is not sure why he is there or what he is meant to be doing. This is when he starts to look elsewhere for another high-octane project. Such leaders are precious in failing businesses, but dangerous in successful ones. Their need for drama in order to maintain their focus can result in them implementing changes where they are not needed and challenging the status quo when stability is necessary.

Many entrepreneurs enjoy the thrill of starting a business and then lose interest once the company is able to stand on its own two feet. The most successful people know that this is the time to move on and bring in a safe pair of hands to focus on steady growth.

If you are seeking your own recipe for success, look at how easily you are able to maintain your focus on the big picture in your company. If this is a constant struggle, learn the lesson and shift your focus to something you can believe in or move to a more suitable environment for you. You cannot fake focus for long.

FOCUS RECIPE

- Mix stubbornness, self-confidence, persistence, flexibility and vision.
- Understand what is actually important to success and focus on that.
- Make sure that what is important is also naturally motivational for you.
- Listen to others whose area of focus is different from yours so you get the complete picture. You cannot focus on everything at once.
- If your efforts do not work first time, do not lose your focus. Simply learn from the experience and apply that learning to your next project. Continue to do this throughout your life.
- Above all, do not get distracted. Keep your sights on your overall objective and make sure that every step you take is intended to bring you closer to that.

REFERENCES

1 Jones, Graham, and Adrian Moorhouse. *Developing Mental Toughness: Gold Medal Strategies for Transforming Your Business Performance*. p.146. Oxford: Spring Hill, 2007.
2 Jones, Graham, and Adrian Moorhouse. *Developing Mental Toughness: Gold Medal Strategies for Transforming Your Business Performance*. p.147. Oxford: Spring Hill, 2007.
3 Jones, Peter. *Tycoon: How to Turn Dreams Into Millions*. p.46. London: Hodder & Stoughton, 2007.
4 Bridge, Rachel. *How I Made It*. p.96. London: Kogan Page, 2005.

Ingredient 3

Steel

Running through the centre of all successful people is a rod of steel. It is this combination of determination and self-belief – this conviction – which enables them to hold their nerve under pressure and ask more of life than do lesser beings. They may have private moments of doubt, but these are fleeting. At their core, successful people are determined about what they want to achieve. They have an inner belief which gives them the confidence to maintain their focus and we saw in the last chapter how important this ingredient is in the recipe for success.

Steel is not necessarily the same as bravery or courage, qualities that are often superimposed on the successful. When I left my job at the BBC, I was told endlessly how brave I was to give up the security of a high-flying job with a respected broadcasting company and head out into the world with nothing but my wits and a business plan. I didn't *feel* brave. I was certainly aware of the significant step I was taking and could easily visualise a doomsday scenario where I had to sell my home and move back in with my parents because it had all gone belly-up. But if I am honest, I enjoyed the feeling that I was taking a risk and following my instincts. It gave me a buzz because I also knew, deep down, that I could make it work. I didn't know *how* exactly, but trusted myself to have the qualities necessary to make my business a success, to be able to navigate my way around or through any obstacle I encountered.

What makes successful people different from those who are paralysed by their fears is that they have steel. Even when confronted with a huge potential danger (losing their home, losing their business, losing their position in society), they don't freak out under pressure. They know what they or their product is worth and they will back it even when other people tell them it is bound to fail. They survive rough financial periods, even bankruptcy, without losing their drive. They put themselves into new and uncomfortable situations and enjoy it! Tennis champion Martina Navratilova summed this up as 'just go out there and do what you've got to do'. No questions. No hesitation.

Let's take Jack Welch as an example. As CEO of US giant corporation General Electric he believed the way to continually upgrade the quality of his organisation was to sack the staff who fell into the lowest-performing 10 per cent each year. Inevitably each year, the bottom 10 per cent was better than the previous year, but out they went. People who had felt safe and secure two or three years earlier were now in the danger zone.

For some staff, this was motivating – what more powerful way to stay focused on excellence than to see people below you lose their jobs each year? If you are motivated by challenge, pressure and expectation, this is the perfect environment. The chaff is continually removed, meaning you get to work with increasingly high-performing colleagues. But if you don't find this kind of 'threat' motivational, you could feel it created an environment of fear, of blame and of individualism. Why would anyone try to help poor performers? The more poor performers there are, the safer your job. Why would managers invest time grooming their team to develop greater skills when they could be creating the guy that puts them out of a job?

Nevertheless, this is what Welch believed at his core. He knew the downsides but felt the upsides were more powerful. His 'steel' meant that he would not budge on this. And, because he believed in himself so completely, he had no need to hide the honest truth of what he was doing. He believed in it and stood by it, no matter what.

For industrial designer and entrepreneur James Dyson, steely determination manifested itself in an ambition which many people believed was sheer madness. 'This project is dead from the neck up,' a Hotpoint executive said when Dyson offered them his vacuum cleaner technology in 1982. He started working on the idea in 1978 and produced his first Dual Cyclone machine in 1993. That's a long time to work on a project with no guarantee of success, but by May 2001 Dyson was responsible for 29 per cent of the vacuum cleaner market by volume and 52 per cent by value.

The same was true for Tim Smit, the visionary behind the Eden Project. When he announced that he was going to take a few acres of a disused former quarry, build a series of greenhouses promoting environmental issues and turn it into one of the biggest tourist destinations in the UK, you can imagine what his prospective investors said. But his sheer unflinching commitment and belief were so powerful that the investors handed over the money. Today it is the third most popular admission-charging visitor attraction in the UK . . . and it is in Cornwall. Only the London Eye and the Tower of London surpass it in popularity.

What distinguishes the individuals described in this chapter is that they are genuinely sure of themselves, even though they may have moments of human frailty. Star Maker Lucy Harris, a headhunter with The Ashton Partnership, believes that successful people have the mindset to push themselves further than other people:

> They are comfortable and self-aware that they are the best in their game and know how to use that as a skill. They stick with their plan, they ignore comment and they reassure themselves that they are always doing the best they can.

THE EXPECTANCY EFFECT

A person's *belief* that they are right may be more powerful as an ingredient for success than actually *being* right. As Henry Ford put it, 'Whether you believe you can do a thing or not, you are right.'

This is called the 'expectancy effect' – events that we expect to occur are more likely to occur. Psychological tests on people intending to give up smoking, for instance, show that those who believe they can do it are more likely to succeed. The expectation of success spurs belief, and this belief has a real effect on the outcome. Those who are most successful at this have an 'internal locus of control'. This means they believe that what happens to them in their life is a direct consequence of their own actions rather than luck or the actions of other people. Because people like Welch, Dyson and Smit believe they can make things happen (and that only they are responsible if they fail to make things happen), they know that the outcome of their life is completely in their own hands. Blend that with ambition and you have a powerful motivational force to take action, to follow through and stick with a plan no matter what other people might think and no matter what other obstacles come into your path.

It is this internal locus of control which enables successful people to achieve success even during difficult times. While many businesses would batten down the hatches during times of economic instability, those who believe down to their core that only they control their destiny are likely to turn economic downturns into opportunities to grow.

GRITTY DETERMINATION

Of course, successful people are human too, and suffer moments of doubt, which Enabler Vicki Day has seen a lot of:

> Sometimes there is a lack of self-esteem. It is such a bizarre thing when you get them in a private moment. But maybe that

is also related to their success. Maybe they are saying, 'I'll show everyone that I am good', sticking two fingers up at everyone else. It is such a contradiction.

Star Maker Lucy Harris believes this vulnerability is also part of the recipe for success:

> The people I see aren't always thick-skinned. Sometimes I believe their skin needs to get tougher. But if they do show a vulnerability in some way, it's only because of a lack of experience, not a lack of confidence. And they are more wonderful because of this quality.

In the privacy of the changing room, image consultant and Enabler, Sharon Connolly, sees what these executives are afraid to show the rest of the world – that they are human too:

> They are just normal people who want to look good and are scared about making the wrong impression. Many are scared to show people what they are really like. I show them a red tie or a purple shirt and they say, 'I couldn't!' They know that whatever they do, they will draw attention to themselves. So we tend to do it over a period of months or years. No matter how successful or business-focused people are, there is nothing that gives them more confidence than being noticed by the opposite sex.

Angela Duckworth of the University of Pennsylvania has led a series of studies in to what she calls 'grit' and believes that 'gritty' people are more likely to achieve success in school, work and other areas because their passion and commitment help them to cope with the inevitable obstacles. Even intelligence and talent take a back seat to grit.[1]

In order to measure which candidates were most likely to survive the first summer of training at West Point, a 'grit' questionnaire was completed by all 1,223 cadets due to enter the class of 2008. It found that 'grit' was the single best yardstick for predicting who would survive the academy's first weeks. High-school class rank, SAT scores, athletic experience and faculty appraisal scores were nowhere near as accurate a predictor as the 'grit' study. 'Sticking with West Point doesn't have as much to do with how smart you are as your character,' Duckworth concluded.

From the age of five, John Savage knew he would have no ordinary job. A self-described 'street urchin' in the years after the Second World War (his father had died in the war and, as a result, John lived in significant poverty), he watched local men coming home from work each day, and was convinced that he would never follow in their footsteps.

Now, as Chief Executive of GWE Business West and a committed mentor to upcoming talent, he says that determination is what sets the successful apart:

> Julius Caesar had an uncanny belief in himself, despite the fact that he was epileptic. Churchill wasn't a natural top man, but knew from his childhood that he was going to be called on to make a big contribution. I knew, from watching the men leaving work at the Woolwich Arsenal, that would never be me. I am from very ordinary stock, but I found that everywhere I went I ended up leading. I didn't set out to do that and I love being in circumstances where I haven't got to do that. But it may come down to the fact that I am decisive. I know there is an answer and I know what needs to be done.

OPTIMISM

One of the necessary elements of 'steel' is optimism – high achievers tend to be optimistic, which helps them to stick with an idea even when there are tough obstacles to overcome. Keith Simonton of the University of California at Davis says:

> They just really believe in the end that they're going to win, and until they do, they're just going to keep on pushing, keep on making the phone calls, writing the letters, whatever they have to do.[2]

In one rather unpleasant piece of research, three dogs were used to explore the importance of optimism to success. The first dog was administered a series of electric shocks, but was able to turn them off by pushing a panel with his nose. The second dog was given the same shocks as the first but with no means of escaping. The third dog was not given any shocks at all. Then all three dogs were placed in a box divided in to two compartments, separated by a low barrier. When the dogs were given another shock, all they had to do to escape was jump over the barrier. The first and third dog did just that. But the second one, who had been taught he had no power to change his situation, just lay down and continued to take the shocks.[3]

Successful people never lie down and take a shock. They know they will be able to find a way forward. And, of course, the more they believe this, the more obstacles they overcome and the more they gain evidence that they are right.

Top PA Deborah Meredith has worked alongside many senior executives. An Enabler who only lets the very deserving through to see her boss, says she never saw self-doubt in the most successful people she worked with:

> These are people who believe they can do it, they believe they deserve it, they believe they can deliver no matter what it takes. Those who have doubts don't achieve as highly as those who say, 'Yes, we can do that.' Those who don't believe

tell their team, 'Let's do our best.' They are already giving everyone an excuse not to achieve.

In Chapter 7 we'll be looking at the thorny issue of talent and whether having any particularly outstanding skill is part of the recipe for success. But certainly research shows that compared to intelligence, grit, determination and steel are more powerful predictors of success, which is why it is surprising that parents (and society at large) still value academic achievement more highly than effort. In fact, one of the greatest impediments to developing this rod of steel may be influential adults who focus their attention on intelligence over all other qualities.

In one series of studies at Stanford University, it was shown that children who were praised for their intelligence cared more about grades than about learning. When these children experienced a failure, they lost motivation, compared to their peers who had been praised for effort. When children who are praised for their intelligence fail, they no longer believe that they are intelligent and they lose hope. Those who are praised for effort are often energised in the face of difficulty. Employers still tend to look for academic qualifications (a degree, post-graduate diploma, good grades) when recruiting rather than evidence of steely determination through difficulty (e.g. climbing one of the great peaks or overcoming personal challenges), thereby reinforcing this emphasis on intelligence and overlooking the huge value of tenacity.[4]

SELF-BELIEF

Professor Graham Jones and Adrian Moorhouse have researched what they refer to as 'mental toughness' – the state of mind which differentiates top sporting performers from those who compete but never quite make the grade. Through their study of elite performers they discovered that sustained high performance relies in part on having strong self-belief and motivation.

Adrian Moorhouse was brought up in a family where personal responsibility was a powerful value. His father was self-made, having left school at 14, and always taught his boys that through hard work they could achieve whatever they set out to achieve. Believing in your qualities and abilities, and being determined to succeed means the battle is half won.[5]

And what does this mentally tough state of mind enable successful individuals to do? Jones and Moorhouse have found that this mental attitude gives exceptional performers the desire and ability to:

- **set and achieve stretching goals;**
- **take and learn from criticism;**
- **establish a balanced perspective on strengths and weaknesses, and to tackle the weaknesses head on;**
- **take risks;**
- **make decisions without fear of being wrong;**
- **control potentially debilitating fear;**
- **bounce back from setbacks with renewed focus and effort;**
- **create a positive future;**
- **provide a strong foundation for dealing with pressure.**

Clearly, this finding applies not only to sportspeople, but to people working in any field. Some of our top entrepreneurs have taken this so far that they have very little in the way of academic achievement to show for themselves, relying almost entirely on 'steel'. Richard Branson and Alan Sugar did not go to university. Mark Zuckerberg, the founder of Facebook, dropped out of Harvard University when the business began to take off. *Dragons' Den's* Duncan Bannatyne left school at 15 with no 'O' levels. In the corporate world, it is tougher to get to the top without a classic education, but, as the evidence here shows, the right degree won't guarantee you a place at the board.

Key Holder Phil Taylor believes that, even in the corporate world, more importance should be placed on personal qualities like 'steel' rather than focusing only on academic achievement:

> There is much research and evidence available to suggest that successful leaders tend to be people who have overcome some level of hardship or challenge in their life, be it professional or personal.
>
> Ideally, of course, you are looking for both qualities – intellectual capacity *and* proof of determination, grit and the tenacity to overcome challenges that get thrown before us. I always give credit to people who have taken difficult choices ahead of the easy route in their personal careers, such as leaving the workforce to enhance their education or take on a challenge for themselves in some other area of their life. It can be a sign of clarity of focus and determination.

Without the determination to turn your opportunities into results, your education is no more than a piece of paper. And while this book is certainly not a manifesto for high school drop-outs, having the right degree is optional, whereas having the right mindset for success is not. The only question you should have now is 'Do I want to succeed badly enough?'

STEEL RECIPE
- Believe in yourself and your ability.
- Be optimistic by gathering evidence of your previous successes.
- When all else fails, rely on your gritty determination to keep going.
- Develop an 'internal locus of control' by taking personal responsibility when events turn out well or turn out badly.

- Reward hard work in preference to academic paperwork in yourself and others.
- Say 'I will do it' rather than 'I will try my best'.

REFERENCES

1 *Psychology Today* magazine, Nov/Dec 2005. Article ID: 3910. p.3. (www.psychologytoday.com/articles/index.php?term=pto-20051017–000003&page=3)
2 *Psychology Today* magazine, Nov/Dec 2005. Article ID: 3910. p.5. (www.psychologytoday.com/articles/index.php?term=pto-20051017–000003&page=3)
3 Seligman, Martin E. P. *Learned Optimism: How to change your mind and your life*. New York: Pocket Books, 1998. [From *Developing Mental Toughness*, p.114.]
4 *Psychology Today* magazine, Nov/Dec 2005. Article ID: 3910. pp.3–5. (www.psychologytoday.com/articles/index.php?term=pto-20051017–000003&page=3)
5 Jones, Graham, and Adrian Moorhouse. *Developing Mental Toughness: Gold Medal Strategies for Transforming Your Business Performance*. p.366. Oxford: Spring Hill, 2007.

Ingredient 4

Trust

Steel is, in part, about trusting yourself – knowing that you are capable of success and combining that with the determination to turn that self-trust into results. But what if you are the only one who believes you have what it takes? Can you be successful without the support and trust of others?

As we have already seen, you will need the support of Star Makers, Key Holders and Enablers at the very least. You may also need to manage a team, develop strong relationships with peers, keep your boss on side, deal with customers or clients, relate to other people in your industry, maybe even develop relationships with the media. You can't achieve any of this without our next ingredient: trust.

It is not necessary for people to like you. In fact, the need to be liked may be an obstacle to success. The 'need to please' means you will find it very tough to make good decisions. Wanting everyone to like you will prevent you from being objective when you need to give critical feedback or when you need to persevere despite the cynicism of others and when you become more successful than the people around you and face resentment as a result.

As a motivation, the 'need to please' is potentially very harmful. If you are doing something to make your partner, your parents, your children, your friends or your colleagues happy, your motivation is likely to wane over time and result in high levels of personal stress. You cannot guarantee that your actions will make other people happy.

As we saw in Chapter 2, successful performers focus on what they can control, and you cannot control the happiness of other people.

But while people don't need to like you, they do need to trust you. And if you are able to inspire trust, you will be in the minority. A survey of Americans in 2002 by Golin-Harris, the international public relations company, found that 69 per cent of respondents agreed with the statement: 'I just don't know who to trust any more'. Roughly half of all managers don't trust their leaders and four out of five members of the public have 'only some' or 'hardly any' confidence in people running major corporations.[1] If you are able to get other people to trust you then you are already setting yourself apart as someone special.

GETTING OTHER PEOPLE TO TRUST YOU

Trust means that other people will take risks for you, put themselves out for you and stand by you during difficult times in a more reliable and sustainable way than they would if they simply like you.

Key Holder and serial entrepreneur Oli Barrett needs to make relatively quick decisions about whom to trust when he is approached by someone looking for advice, assistance or a contact:

> There is a lot of gut feel in that decision to trust. If you spend a lot of time with people, you develop an ability to sense bull. I also look at their track record. And I ask myself, 'Does what they are saying make sense in relation to what I've seen?' That's why it is important to be knowledgeable about the area in which you work. If I don't know the first thing about the Web but I am trying to connect people in that field, I am not able to tell whether what I am being told makes sense.

Oli has developed his own mechanism over time for judging whether to trust someone. But all of us get an initial taste of what someone is like by combining the 'feeling' we have about people and the 'evidence' we gather into a powerful guiding force. People may enjoy your company a great deal, but your track record may not back up your claims. Equally, people may have a history of your impressive achievements but can't connect with you on a personal basis.

According to David Maister, one of the *Financial Times* top 40 business thinkers in the world, leaders cannot function without trust. You don't have to manage people directly to be a leader: anyone who is successful leads in one way or another, so this is relevant to you. You may influence minds, you may be an agent of change in your industry or in the world, or you may have people who rely on you for their livelihoods.

Maister identifies four dimensions to trust, three of which increase levels of trust, and one of which reduces them.[2]

- **Credibility** (which is about words). 'I can trust what he says'. This is about tangible, professional expertise, the track record that Oli Barrett mentioned.
- **Reliability** (which is about actions). 'I can trust her to do something'. This is about whether you are dependable and behave in consistent ways. Are you all 'talk' or do you consistently turn your words into results?
- **Intimacy** (which is about emotions). 'I feel comfortable discussing this with that person'. This is about being able to relate to people on a one-to-one basis. This is where our feelings about people are so powerful. Some people make you feel comfortable, safe or inspired; others do not.
- **Self-orientation** (which is about motives). 'What does this person care about?' If the person seems to focus on the other person in the relationship, trust increases. If they are more concerned with themselves and their needs, trust is diminished. Feelings and evidence are in play here. Over time your initial feelings about a person can be questioned as the evidence in their favour or against them builds.

'Trusters', the people looking at you and deciding whether they trust you or not, are making a wide range of calculations constantly about how trustworthy you are. Trust is not static; in the mix are your behaviours, the needs and character of the truster and the situation. All of these can all influence how trustworthy you appear at any one time.

Some trusters are risk intolerant and will only trust people who they believe will offer safety and security. Others enjoy the spiciness of risk and tend to have faith that things will work out. Your own attitude towards risk will be relevant here. If you are a risk-seeker, you will tend to attract other risk-takers or people who believe their own cautionary approach is not serving them well. But people seeking reassurance and facts about what the future holds will find you a 'maverick' . . . and not in a good way.

Equally, people who are well-adjusted and comfortable with themselves and the world, take less time to trust others. They are more open to different flavours, to taking a chance with someone they haven't worked with before. If you have a team of well-adjusted individuals, you are off to a more solid start. However, if your team is poorly adjusted and sees the world as a threatening place, you will need to build trust over a longer period.

I have worked with companies where trust has been seriously damaged by previous generations of managers. In one company (let's call it ABC Manufacturing), a new leadership team was appointed, in the hope that its arrival would be enough to spark a new era. Instead, it met with resistance, cynicism and even obstinacy. This was very confusing for the new senior team at ABC. After all, the members of the team were not responsible for what went before. Everyone had loved them in their previous jobs. And they thought they had communicated well to their new employees how committed they were to turning the company around. But their words landed on stony ground. In fact, the more they communicated, the more negative the response from the shop floor became.

They had arrived in a poorly adjusted environment and had expected trust to be bestowed because they knew their own motivations were genuine. But as long as the only evidence of their commitment was words, they were doing nothing to build trust. It was only when staff began to see actions, and lots of them, did they begin to contemplate the possibility that these leaders really meant what they said. Even then, it took many months of continually being challenged to prove their commitment before the staff started to accept them at their word.

Power is also a factor affecting trust. People in a position of authority are far more likely to trust others because they can always fire them, demote them or make their lives a misery if they are let down. Those without authority are always taking a much greater risk when they trust other people and are, therefore, more cautious. Only when they can see how decisions are made, and that they are made fairly, are powerless individuals able to trust those with more power.

TRUST SHORT-CUTS AND THE NEED TO ACHIEVE

In situations where it is difficult to win people's trust, some leaders try a short-cut, preferring to force or intimidate others into following them. Trust, as we have seen, can take a long time to build if trusters are cautious, poorly adjusted and powerless. Gaining trust in such circumstances involves working tirelessly to challenge assumptions, demonstrate reliability and present results.

We see such short-cuts being attempted on television programmes like *The Apprentice*. Such shows do not allow either the time or the conditions for trust to grow. Leaders for a particular challenge are chosen reluctantly by a group of people who do not want to be led. They want to win, but if they lose, they would prefer to see someone else's head on the block. These are not ideal circumstances for trust to develop. However, the types of behaviour seen on *The Apprentice* are not limited to television portrayals of leadership; they are seen in the workplace too. And such behaviour is motivated, in a large part, by another characteristic commonly found in ambitious people – the need for achievement.

Most people in our culture are taught to value achievement. And for some people, this drive to achieve is innate. They get a particular buzz from achieving and will create opportunities to do so. They will play competitive sports or take part in quizzes as long as there is a prize (a certificate will do) at the end. They pursue work that is competitive, too, and feel better about themselves when they have proof of accomplishment. Often they are identified as 'high potential' by their organisation and put into positions of leadership. Their drive to achieve is expected to inspire those around them and, for a short time, it often does. Research carried out by Harvard psychologist David McClelland in the 1960s initially showed that of the three motivations (the others being affiliation – the need to belong; and power – the need to influence), achievement was the most critical to organisational success. He found that in countries with a high concern for achievement one often saw rapid economic growth. In countries where the concern for achievement dropped, there was often a decline in economic welfare.[3]

However, McClelland also saw that there were drawbacks to such a commitment to achievement. People with this as an innate motivator are sometimes willing to cut corners or even cheat to achieve their goal. One of the reasons levels of trust in the business world are so low is because of ethical failures in companies like Enron and WorldCom. When organisations are led by people motivated by achievement, the ends are often seen to justify the means. Leaders in such cultures rely on a directive or pace-setting style. They either tell people what to do or do it themselves. They do not bother investing the time to generate a culture of trust. And, according to research by Hay Group, reduced trust and morale have a direct impact of productivity and confidence in the management.[4]

In later work, McClelland changed his mind, concluding that

leaders who were motivated by socialised power – the need to help people feel stronger and more capable – were actually most effective. And while pushing and prodding staff can work in the short term, and under certain circumstances, it isn't a strategy that John Savage would promote:

> I have found that you can get the same discipline and the same degree of bravery if you simply enlighten people. You see bullying portrayed on some of these current TV programmes. Why would you want to work in that kind of environment? It clearly does work for some people, but I would contend it doesn't get the best out of them.

Dishonesty is also a huge threat to trust. If, at interview stage, someone demonstrates they cannot be trusted, it leaves a bad taste in the mouth of headhunter Lucy Harris. Her reputation relies on her finding the best candidate for a senior post, fast. She doesn't have patience with people who lack integrity:

> It is not in my nature to block people's way. But if I see dishonesty, I will. Dishonesty comes in many forms. If you are not genuinely interested in taking up an appointment, don't go to the 5th interview and sign the contract and let them think you are going to start, don't string people along. There are huge emotions involved in a senior appointment, huge expectations, companies looking to the future. So what I won't deal with is false emotions.

INSPIRING TRUST

So, if dishonesty is a real no-no when it comes to engendering trust, what qualities are a big yes-yes?

People tend to trust others who seem similar to them. The more we have in common with another person the more we will trust them.

People Like Us share the same values, the same background, the same interests or the same personality traits and therefore we feel we can predict how they will behave in a variety of circumstances. We assume they will behave like us. This is reassuring. Erratic behaviour is unsettling so where we believe we understand each other we feel more secure.

This is not to say that everyone in an organisation or everyone in your circle must be a carbon copy of you. In fact, having a variety of opinions and perspectives is vital to generate fresh ideas and make good decisions (see Chapter 5). However, successful people are able to find connections with others that can make anyone, no matter how diverse they may be in some aspects, feel like they have something in common.

Phil Taylor, Vice President of Human Resources for Mattel, says people might not like you, but if they trust you, you can get things done:

> If you don't have trust you can't engage an organisation. People might not invite you to their wedding but they do trust you and they do respect you. Most people like to be liked but in terms of pursuing a mission I think they understand that it is important to be trusted. They can live with the fact that they might not be loved ... although they would probably prefer one or two around them who love them. It would be very lonely otherwise.

Demonstrating integrity (basically the opposite of the dishonesty Lucy Harris observed) is also vital for developing trust. A good test of integrity is to ask oneself the following questions:

- **If my mother knew everything I was doing, what would she think?**

And:

- **How would I feel if everything I was doing was printed in the newspaper?**[5]

If you have a clear conscience then you are in a positive place for developing trust.

Integrity means holding oneself to a set of high moral principles. So, whatever you say you are going to do, you must do. Overpromising and underdelivering are amongst the most common mistakes which undermine trust. In his research into trust, Robert F. Hurley, professor of management at Fordham University in New York, found that people who were well-intentioned, who cared passionately about their work but were led by their enthusiasm to promise more than they could deliver are not trusted by colleagues because of their poor track records.[6]

It is far better to underpromise and overdeliver. And if you cannot fulfil your promises, explain why honestly and fully.

Literary agent Carole Blake described how one of her authors, on a reading tour of Spain, attended a full day of readings despite having food poisoning. He could easily have spent the day in his hotel room but he did not want to let his hosts down and did not want to imply that the local cuisine was anything but delicious. Consequently Carole and her team know that they can trust him to fulfil his promises. This reflects well on the literary agency as well as the author and therefore Carole is more likely to go out of her way for clients who behave as professionally as this.

One factor which massively increases trust, as we have already seen, is ability. In fact, in many situations, it matters less whether you connect on a personal level with someone than that they know what they are doing (a heart surgeon for instance). However, it is not enough to talk about how talented and effective you are. In fact, such talk tends to undermine credibility. Those who inspire trust demonstrate through their actions what they are capable of.

Executive PA Deborah Meredith says that the most successful

people she has worked with are always trying to improve their performance. They are never complacent about their abilities:

> They are learning from their peers, reading around the subject, they have extensive bookshelves, they take books and articles to a beach with them when they are on holiday, anything that will make them improve. They are interested in personal development, maybe not the way the majority of us would recognise, but they have people they speak to – peers, mentors, a long lunch with someone they respect – they don't have the time for navel gazing but they want to keep on pushing the boundaries.

Sharon Connolly, an image consultant and Enabler who advises influential executives on how to dress, believes that clothes have a powerful impact on how people perceive, and therefore, trust, one another:

> You need to think about who you are trying to impact upon, what you are trying to say about yourself. You need to look as if you are already successful. Some people can do that in jeans and a t-shirt and look wrong in an Armani suit. But I would always suggest you dress a little bit smarter than your counterparts because it makes you look more senior. People have the feeling you are in charge.

How you dress is actually a form of communication. And communication is a valuable tool to improve trust. As we saw earlier, talk without substance is bad for trust. But worse is miscommunication or no communication. People tend to fill the gaps in their knowledge with gossip, rumour or fear. In a company where results are not widely communicated, staff will suspect that leaders have something to hide. Rumours will start about the financial position of the company.

Numbers will be bandied about. People will begin talking about redundancy or receivership. Morale will be affected and eventually so will results. In the worst cases, lack of communication can actually lead to poor results when the company was initially doing quite well.

Leaders regularly underestimate what communication actually entails and are then surprised when their staff distrust them. Sending out e-mails or reports which are not read or are difficult to navigate is not communication. The very word implies getting the message *across*. Successful people are always checking what messages are being received and ensuring that they are understood completely.

And this is vital outside the world of big business too. Whether your ambition is to be a movie star, a millionaire author or mother-of-the-year, honest and sensitive communication will buy you a lot of trust. None of us is perfect and few of us would be completely happy with having every detail of our work or life published in the press for our Mum to see. But how we communicate when things go wrong – when our cake fails to rise as it were – will contribute to whether or not we survive the exposé.

TRUST RECIPE

- You may not be to everyone's taste personally, but people do have to trust you if you are going to be successful.
- Understand who your trusters are and what qualities they need to see in you before they are ready to trust you.
- Do not let your need for achievement overpower your personal recipe.
- Do not commit acts which you would not want your loved ones or the press to know about.
- Be honest in your dealings.

- Build genuine rapport by finding connections between yourself and other people.
- Underpromise and overdeliver. If you cannot deliver, explain why honestly.
- Hone your ability so that you have the capability to do what needs to be done.
- Communicate effectively but concisely: aim for quality over quantity.

REFERENCES

1 Hurley, Robert F. 'The Decision to Trust'. p.55. *Harvard Business Review*, September 2006.
2 http://davidmaister.com/podcasts.archives/5/55
3 Fontaine, Mary H., Ruth L. Mallory, and Scott W. Spreier. 'Leadership Run Amok: The Destructive Potential of Overachievers'. p.76. *Harvard Business Review*, June 2006.
4 Fontaine, Mary H., Ruth L. Mallory, and Scott W. Spreier. 'Leadership Run Amok: The Destructive Potential of Overachievers'. p.74. *Harvard Business Review*, June 2006.
5 Gardner, Howard. 'The Ethical Mind.' p.56. Harvard Business Review, March 2007
6 Hurley, Robert F. 'The Decision to Trust.' p.59. *Harvard Business Review*, September 2006.

Ingredient 5

Kitchen Cabinet

All good cooks have a well-stocked larder full of complementary ingredients and staples. A meal might be built around a lovely roast beef or fillet of salmon, but you need the potatoes, the greens and the seasoning to make it into a feast.

Without taking the analogy too far, no one is a success all by themselves. No one is so multi-talented, so versatile, so perfect that they can reach the top without support and help from other people. All successful people have an overview of their business and their industry (as we will see in Chapter 8), but it is impossible to be a specialist at every aspect. The successful people we have heard of might be the headliners – your Anita Roddicks or your Donald Trumps. But behind the scenes, these individuals rely heavily on a formal and informal team of experts, all as talented and skilful in their own area of expertise as the star.

So far, the ingredients needed for your recipe are found within you. But the 'kitchen cabinet' is an ingredient you have to find outside of yourself and getting your hands on the right calibre and mixture is key to your success.

We all have limitations and successful people know their talents and the limits of those talents. They focus as much of their time and energy as possible on the parts of the business that they excel in and they focus on their areas of strength rather than their areas of weakness. Of course, they have to learn about aspects of their business which may not turn them on and they have to develop skills outside their natural talent, but you will always find some who are brilliant communicators yet hopeless at the number crunching, others who have a knack for buying and selling but can't communicate to a large audience and a few who are original thinkers with brilliant ideas but get bored quickly when it comes to running a business long term. They fill in the gaps in their own ability by finding or developing other people. As Phil Taylor puts it:

> There are very few things you can achieve on your own. You need to gather data, consider the input of others. Top people have the ability to surround themselves with other talent, with smart people, with people who also share their passion. They engage themselves with people who can help them achieve.

WHERE IS THE GAP?

The purpose of your 'kitchen cabinet' – typically an informal group of trusted advisors – is to fill in the gaps in your own ability and knowledge so that, with their insight and expertise, you become invincible. It is time to take a long hard look at what your natural talents are, which may be different to asking yourself what you enjoy. It may even be different to asking what you are good at. We can learn to be good at activities that are not natural talents. All trainee chefs spend time in every part of the kitchen – they will learn how to make desserts, how to prep vegetables, how to make sauces, how to bake bread, how to cook fish, but most will find a section where they excel. They will be flexible enough to stand in for a colleague if necessary, but they will never excel in that section as they do in their own.

I enjoy playing the piano, but I am not particularly good at it. And I am quite good at carrying out research, but it will never be a natural talent, simply something I have learnt to do because I appreciate its importance. However, while we might not always excel at what we enjoy and might have ability outside our natural strengths, we generally enjoy and are good at those tasks where we have an innate gift (there are some exceptions which we will learn about in Chapter 7 on Talent). The most successful people build their careers around their natural talents and passions. And then they build a cabinet of people with different natural talents from their own.

WORK STYLE PREFERENCES

Most people have quite clear innate work preferences. According to work by TMS Development International Ltd,[1] most of us have ways we prefer to relate to one another, ways we prefer to gather and use information, ways we make decisions and ways we organise ourselves and other people.

For instance, most of us have a tendency to be introvert or extrovert. This is not the same as being shy or confident, but refers to the way we relate to other people. Are you someone who prefers to work alone and think things through for yourself, or are you someone who prefers to talk about ideas while working alongside other people? This will give you clues as to whether you are introvert or extrovert. Equally, some people prefer to work with facts, details and pre-tested ideas while others prefer generating their own ideas and working with more ambiguous situations. This indicates whether they are more practical or more creative.

Some people make decisions in an analytical way, setting up objective decision-making criteria and choosing solutions which meet those criteria. Other people rely largely on their gut and make decisions based on their beliefs, often finding the evidence to support their view afterwards. And some people are more structured and organised, having timescales and deadlines in order to resolve issues. Others prefer more flexibility, which means they can adapt or modify their plans as they go to suit changing situations.

Depending on your preferences, you will need to construct a

cabinet which contains the full variety of personality types. If you are a gut-feel decision-maker, you will want to ensure you have some analytical decision-makers around you. If you simply ignore the facts (or ignore the people who give you the facts), you may risk making wildly risky decisions. Alternatively, if you tend to pore over details for long periods, you will need people who can advise you that the time for decision making has come. As Ralph Larsen, Chair and CEO of Johnson & Johnson put it, 'At the point when you've gathered enough data to be 99.9 per cent certain that the decision you are about to make is correct, that decision has become obsolete.'[2]

The right balance between assessing the facts and acting fast is vital to success. Few individuals have the capacity to do both with equal vigour and your cabinet can help you to get the balance right. And the same is true for all the other qualities. It is fantastic to be an enthusiastic extrovert who encourages other people to get behind your vision and start talking about possibilities. But if that is the prevalent style in your business, there isn't enough room for quiet contemplation: there's clearly a lot of talk going on, but how much action? Ideas may be thrown about but no one sits down long enough with one of them to think properly about their viability. And anyone further down the hierarchy of the business who is a different type from you will feel confused by your behaviour. Having people close to you who have a variety of styles means that there is always someone in the business or linked to the business whom those different personalities can connect with.

EXTERNAL INSIGHT

This leads to the second consideration. It may not be possible, nor wise, for you to construct your perfect cabinet from within your business. According to Saj-nicole A. Joni,[3] the higher leaders rise, the more impact their decisions have on greater numbers of people, which means they are in greater need of advisers who can provide honest and expert opinions.

The problem is that that they tend to look to a small number of people on their staff who they have grown to trust over a period of years. And this small network relies very heavily on the leader for their future well-being. No matter how great their expertise, they will always be influenced in their advice by its impact on their own lives. Will anyone give you their honest opinion if that means their job will become redundant? Will anyone tell give you feedback if they know this will result in a smaller budget for their department next year?

A corporate lawyer recently told me that her bonus was not linked to company profits, which is very common in her field because a lawyer's advice should not be based on whether a course of action will grow the business, but on whether it is legal and ethical. Sometimes her advice will inhibit company growth and she needs to be able to express this opinion objectively without concern for the effect that company stagnation will have on her annual bonus. That's why some of your best advisers will come from outside your business, people who have no personal stake in the advice they give and are therefore in a position of structural trust.

In her article 'The Geography of Trust', Joni writes '"Nations don't have friends; they have interests," said the late French president Charles de Gaulle. Leaders do have friends, but the greater the leaders' power, the more interested those friends are likely to become. And the more interested those friends become, the less leaders should rely solely upon their counsel.'[4]

Advisers in positions of the highest structural trust are generally found outside organisations in order to ensure they are not tainted by self-interest or the culture of the organisation or industry. It is one of the reasons I rarely work with media companies. My background in journalism means that my own feelings about the industry cloud my objectivity. I have rather strong views about the way the news is gathered and the way stories are presented and found the culture of the broadcasting companies I worked for actually suffocated creativity and originality. These views make it rather difficult for me to remain non-judgemental when I work with news editors and broadcasting company executives.

In a pharmaceutical company or a manufacturing business, however, I can apply my expertise without becoming overly sensitive to the implications of that expertise. I have a sense of perspective which isn't muddied by my own personal experience, unlike those who work in the business. And, because I won't be affected by the final decision, I can be honest in my opinions.

FROM TRUSTEE TO TRUSTER

So, in addition to objectivity, what other qualities should you consider when building a 'kitchen cabinet'? Obviously, we are looking for people who meet the same criteria as we ourselves need to meet in order to gain trust. In Chapter 4, we saw what it takes to win the trust of others. Now you are the one wondering whom to trust, so the same considerations apply.

You are looking for people who are technically competent and reliable, qualities that you can only judge over time. Invariably, you are also looking for people whom you connect with at some level. This is something that Key Holder Oli Barrett, whose primary role is connecting people who may be able to assist one another in business, values in his business relationships:

The smartest entrepreneurs have recruited people who are in love with the company's main cause. The old cliché is that opposites attract. I am not sure that's true – you have to have sufficient ingredients in common to get on, but bring different skill sets to bear. But it is important to have like-minded people in a business, not necessarily to be best friends, but to have good will and affection which keeps you going in tough times. You need people around you who are going to make your business life easier and who make you want to go to work.

One way to develop your cabinet is to 'build it yourself'. This is the approach taken by mentor and strategist John Savage, Chairman of the United Bristol Healthcare Trust and holder of other significant board roles. He believes the best way to surround yourself with a solid team is to develop your own talent. Even when making senior appointments, he still commits to working with the individual to hone their abilities to suit his and the organisation's needs. As an Enabler, he believes most people need help in order to perform to a high level:

> You can't run an organisation on your own. Even the most gifted of people are not fully equipped to do the job. But they will be if you work with them. You can't run a hospital of 7,000 employees unless you allow people to make a few mistakes and learn from those mistakes, knowing they have the protection of the Board so that their mistakes are not devastating for us. I remember someone I worked with getting very frustrated at me when I told her to grow up. She threw back at me, 'Yeah, give me the manual.' And I realised that's what you have to do; you have to show people. Animals are programmed very well, they have good instincts. Humans have instincts too, but with a lot of things you have to show them what needs to be done.

Of course, the DIY approach does mean you risk only exposing yourself to opinions developed in your own shadow. We tend to be greatly influenced by those who have moulded us, protected us and given us a leg-up. How do you ensure that you aren't surrounded by a cabinet of yes-men?

It is all about how you mould and develop your team, according to Enabler Deborah Meredith:

> Top people need their team, they need its insight. In order to

deliver their role and properly carry out their responsibilities, they need others. No one knows everything. And they often choose people who are very strong who they can identify with. Sometimes there are clashes, but because everyone is a strong person they can stand up to each other. Give one of these leaders a yes-man and he'll walk all over him. Knowing that people will stand up to you builds respect. But even though the people I have worked for were key people, they never regarded themselves as the kingpin; they knew they were delivering as a team.

The downside of developing such a strong team of successful people within your business is that they may eventually leave you to lead their own project or organisation.

In my first BBC job, I had an inspirational boss called Tony Fish. He attracted fresh new talent straight out of journalism school to work with him at BBC Newcastle, the radio station which serves the North East of England. He knew that he wouldn't keep many of his prodigies for long – many would be attracted to the bright lights of London. But for the time he had them, he would have access to their talent, their enthusiasm and their creativity. And because he was always generous in helping them to develop their talent and supportive in their ambitions, people often stayed at the station for a little longer than they would have done otherwise.

Those of us who work in a small business or a situation where we work primarily on our own are protected slightly from this phenomenon because most of our cabinet will be made up of external advisers. For instance, I have a coach, a PA, a book-keeper, an agent, various mentors and a network of business owners in my cabinet. Those who are paid to be part of that team are all freelance and do not rely on me solely for their income. They have other clients and can therefore afford to be quite honest in their feedback to me, and the rest are rewarded in a purely reciprocal way – I give them advice and they return the favour. However, there is still turnover even in a completely external cabinet. People move location, they change direction or they just get too busy to invest their time.

Successful people understand that there will be turnover and are always adjusting the membership of their cabinet to fill the gaps that are left by departed members. Some advisers, especially those from outside their organisation, may remain in their circle for many years, even decades. Others will gain valuable experience under their tutelage and then move on.

Enabler Vicki Day, who provides PR services for retail professionals, says the most successful leaders encourage ambition, even if that means they lose their best people:

> Real entrepreneurs and leaders encourage other people to be entrepreneurs and leaders. Stuart Rose [at M&S] has this team of key people, Charlie Wilson and Steven Sharp. They all nurture and grow other people. Some of these top people actually go through a lot of staff because they don't so much surround themselves with successful people but they allow other people to become successful with them and then move on.

A STRONG CABINET

It is never too soon to start building your 'kitchen cabinet'. If you are still on your way up in whatever field you hope to succeed, it will be easier for you to find people in positions of structural trust. You are responsible for fewer people's livelihood and, therefore, people can be honest with you without risk to themselves. In addition, relationships forged now can grow in strength with time (as long as nothing changes the nature of the relationship, e.g. you become the boss of someone who used to be a peer).

In maintaining a cabinet you must always keep your wits about you, never becoming overly reliant on individuals who may, as circumstances change, have a huge amount of sensitive information and little compunction to respect its confidential nature. On the other hand, trusting no one leaves you isolated and vulnerable. You will be tripped up by your own weaknesses and no-one will be obliged to point out why this keeps happening.

KITCHEN CABINET RECIPE

- Just as a slab of prime rib isn't a dish on its own, you can't be a success without help, advice and support.
- Take time to stew over your own natural strengths and weaknesses.
- Sprinkle your cabinet with people who mask your weaknesses.
- Look beyond your backyard for cabinet members with a high degree of structural trust.
- Sift out people who do not meet your rigorous guidelines when choosing who to trust.
- Be prepared for some cabinet members to evaporate and be willing to add new ones that are to your taste.
- Stir your cabinet occasionally to remove cabinet members who no longer meet your needs.

REFERENCES

1 See www.tmsdi.com for more information
2 Hayashi, Alden M. 'When to Trust Your Gut'. p.3. *Harvard Business Review*, February 2001.
3 Joni, Saj-nicole A. 'The Geography of Trust'. p.82 *Harvard Business Review*, March 2004
4 Joni, Saj-nicole A. 'The Geography of Trust'. p.83. *Harvard Business Review*, March 2004.

Ingredient 6

Politics

As the 'kitchen cabinet' concept is often used in a political context, it seems appropriate now to turn to (what can be) the sour taste of our next ingredient: politics. Politics certainly has a bad name – it is associated with lying, misleading and selfish motivations. We suspect that decisions made in a political environment are based on the power and influence of unknown parties behind the scenes and there is a lack of transparency. Politics corrupts even the most moral of individuals.

This may be why many of my more junior clients have stated that, if promotion within the organisation means 'playing politics', they don't want to progress. They fear they will inevitably have to sacrifice their integrity, forget their roots and turn their backs on their friends in the organisation if they step up to the next level and, unsurprisingly, they are reluctant to pay this price. Consequently, many talented, energetic, ethical, original thinkers exclude themselves from the senior ranks and business is all the poorer for that.

Like it or not, politics is a reality in our world. It isn't just found in the corridors of power at Westminster or in the corridors of the 29th floor in mega-corporations but in every industry and every walk of life.

Star Maker and literary agent Carole Blake accepts that she and her authors need to have a political awareness:

You have to be able to play the game even if you hate it. Authors have to do it when they are expected to turn into publicity animals to promote a book and then go back into a quiet room to write the next one. I do it when I am trying to get a new publisher interested in one of my authors or when I am talking to the heads of the bookselling chains. You can't be explicit about it but you are constantly ratcheting up the game. If one of my author's editors leaves a publishing house, you get lots of approaches from other editors for that writer. I think, 'If my author isn't happy by this time next year, I will move him.' And the competing editors are thinking the same. They will make a note of the departure and call me in a few months to see how things are going. People saying they won't play politics is ludicrous. It's just working with other people. We all do it when we decide who to say hello to in the morning.

We've all met people who are so determined not to be political that they sabotage themselves and their ability to get things done – a colleague who insists on 'speaking his mind' whenever he gets in front of the boss, a friend who tells you everything that is wrong with you whether you asked for her opinion or not, a family member who refuses to 'make nice' at a big get-together. Equally though, we all know people who are so duplicitous that it is impossible to figure out where they stand and what they think – the colleague who sucks up to anyone with power, the friend who bitches behind someone's back and is all air-kisses in their company, the family member who sets up conflict and then stands back to watch the sparks fly.

All the experts I asked about politics for this book said that it was naïve to think you could be successful without this ingredient. But perhaps it is important to clarify our terms and make a distinction between 'good politics' and 'bad politics'. Just as the best wild mushrooms can transform even a slice of toast into a feast and the worst wild mushrooms can kill you, 'good politics' entails the art of persuasion, the skill of the negotiator and the talent of the long-view strategist ... while 'bad politics' entails the manipulation, back-stabbing and wheeler-dealing of the smoke-filled room. Phil Taylor from Mattel believes getting politics right means looking at the definition of the word:

> Of course, it depends what you mean by politics. My definition of politics is thinking about what you want to communicate. You have a purpose and a message and a mission and you need to engage other people to bring that to fruition. You think about how you engage others, where are their thoughts at this point in time, why do they have certain opinions and how do I communicate and engage with them in a way that helps me bring about the right thing to do, as I believe it to be. The perception is that politics is about people scheming and conniving – that it has something Machiavellian about it and some people do behave in that way. But if it is about engaging others to do what you think is the right thing, then you have to be political to be successful. If you are trying to get a corporation to invest millions of dollars, you need to think about how to get your message across, and why they might object so that you can address them effectively. If that is political, then yes, you need to be good at it.

WHY ARE WE POLITICAL?

Most walks of life are competitive. That is because hierarchies are pyramids: there are fewer people at the top than further down. As some people rise up the ranks, most inevitably have to stay where they are or opt out of the game (only to join another hierarchy somewhere else).

While it might be fairest to promote people (or offer a book deal or a recording contract) based purely on ability, a number of other considerations are also taken into account. No one can achieve any level of success if they are completely unknown. Someone – a Star

Maker, Key Holder or Enabler – has to have heard of them, rate them and be willing to assist them. Someone with more power or influence has to open a door, put their name forward or recommend them to the decision-maker. Ability to do the job will be valued, of course, but other considerations might be *more* valued. As we have already seen, someone who respects the etiquette of the environment by speaking appropriately or dressing acceptably, or someone who inspires trust, might have the edge over someone who does not. And someone who understands politics and can play the game effectively will be able to influence, impress and convince key decision-makers, meaning they are more likely to be seen as the winning candidate for a job or to have the winning argument in a case of conflicting views.

Writing in the *Harvard Business Review* in 1970, the academic Abraham Zaleznik put it like this:

> Organisations are political structures which . . . provide plat-
> forms for the expression of individual interests and motives.
> The development of careers . . . depends on the accumulation
> of power as the vehicle for transforming individual interests
> into activities which influence other people.[1]

In times of recession, the ability to play politics may be even more vital to survival. Those who keep their jobs aren't just lucky, they have stared reality in the face and made plans for the future. Acting like a survivor by putting on a confident and cheerful face can mean, when jobs are lost, you aren't axed. While everyone prefers working with a personable superstar to an incompetent jerk, when people need help getting a job done, they'll choose a congenial colleague over one who is more capable but less lovable.[2] Choosing which face to present to your workmates may seem Machiavellian, but is much more about staying positive so that you are in a position to influence how things turn out in the future.

Another reason why politics may be more common in today's work environment is that the days of 'command and control' leadership are gone. Leaders can't just tell subordinates what to do any more (well, they may try, but it won't work for long). Employees want to know why, they want to be convinced of the arguments, they want to be won over. Therefore, people with differing views about the right course of action need to conduct a campaign of persuasion, to create a powerful constituency within their organisation who will press for their course of action. This might mean winning around the majority of the staff, or it might mean winning around one or two people on the board or a small group of informal centres of influence, who then, in turn, convince their people to back you. And that's politics, folks.

Enabler John Savage works in a political environment with both a small 'p' and a big 'P':

> Politics is about understanding the regimes and pressures that make things happen. So in local government there will be protocols and established ways of doing things which are, to me, very obviously wrong. I believe we could cut a third of the cost of local authority provisions without a shadow of a doubt if it weren't for this culture. However, I've spent a lot of time understanding the culture and going along with it in order to, at the right moment, get them enlightened or to use the influence I have to make them change. That's playing politics. Rather than being straightforward and saying you are wrong, don't do it, I would say, 'Well, OK, tell me more about it,' and I would enable things to happen on that route and we would get there in the end.

IT'S HUMAN NATURE

Another way that you and I actually create political organisations is that we demand that our leaders be political in order to protect or promote our interests. A leader relies on the authority granted to him or her by their formal position and by his or her followers. Leaders cannot operate effectively if they lose their position or if their people are not behind them (as I often say, you're not leading if no one else is following).

Leaders can't just say to their team, 'I agree with this course of action even though you won't like it and some of you will lose your job.' They have to manage the message they give to us. I once worked with a company – let's call it Champion Microsystems – on its internal communication strategy. Feedback from the staff convinced senior managers that they must improve the way they communicated. Their first instinct was to just tell their employees the truth, uncensored and unmanaged. The message would have been:

> We don't trust you and you don't trust us. Most of us want to work somewhere else and you probably do too. And we're not confident that the situation is going to improve.

The managers decided not to do this. In fact, they decided that instead of communicating more they were going to start by listening more, so they organised 'town hall' meetings for staff to express their concerns and held one-to-one sessions and focus groups to show they were interested in their people. Only then did they start transmitting their own message to the staff, but it was a positive one, showing appreciation for the input they had received and outlining their strategy for acting on this information as well as their own ideas. Trust began to improve and so did results.

At the same time, our leaders need to manage the message they get from us when they communicate it to their own peers and superiors. They realise that telling the whole blunt truth is unlikely to get the desired result, and the important thing is to get the result. The means matter less. A leader cannot say, 'Don't cut my team in half, cut someone else's team in half, otherwise my team won't like me any more.' The leader has to find some more convincing argument which looks as though he or she is interested in the common good. This is just another form of politics.

IF YOU DON'T USE IT . . .

According to Harvard Business School professor Abraham Zaleznik, we all have a need to use the power we possess to its fullest extent. In addition to power coming from our position and our attractiveness (how much people respect and like us and are willing to follow us), it also comes from the authority we gain as a result of experience and track record. We internalise that power and start to see ourselves differently as a result of that. It becomes part of our self-esteem, how we value ourselves:

> The individual knows he has power . . . and is willing to risk his personal esteem to influence others . . . The individual must perform *and* get results. If he fails to do either, an attrition occurs in his power base.[3]

In other words, if you don't use it, you lose it. If you have power and the ability to influence, but stand by and do nothing as people around you are crying out for assistance, they will quickly turn on you and your ability to influence them in future is severely damaged. Your track record is tarnished and you have to work hard to win people back over. Part of your authority is gone and you have to start all over again to rebuild it.

So, there is a constant pressure to pitch in with some cause or other. You need to be seen to be doing something so that, when you really need it, your power is still intact. And as long as you continue to get results, people will continue to reward you with authority and influence. It is a vicious circle which perpetuates political behaviour.

GOOD POLITICS, BAD POLITICS

It is important to distinguish between the different types of behaviour which characterise 'good politics' and 'bad politics'.

There has been a lot of emphasis on 'authentic leadership' in recent years, the belief that by being yourself you are more effectively able to motivate, inspire and connect with the people around you. Humans are very intuitive and will sense when someone is playing a role that isn't really an expression of themselves. We tend not to trust this kind of person and, when people get politics wrong, it is partly because they have tried to be all things to all people . . . none of which is a true expression of their authentic self.

But as we have already seen, speaking your mind on every issue in a blunt and unmanaged way can be a highly ineffective way to bring about the changes you think are necessary. So 'good politics' entails some 'flexibility' in your personal style. In their study of authentic leadership, organisational development experts Rob Goffee and Gareth Jones explain:

> The challenge of authentic leadership is finding common ground with the people you seek to recruit as followers. This means you will have to present different faces to different audiences, a requirement that many people find hard to square with authenticity. But, as Shakespeare recognised long ago, 'All the world's a stage . . . and one man in his time plays many parts.'[4]

The difficulty is getting the right balance between adapting your style in order to effectively bring about change, and leaving people with the sense they have been tricked.

'Good politics' means looking at yourself and identifying the parts of your authentic being which particular groups of followers are looking for. It might be something in your past which people can connect with, a motivation you share, a sense of humour, an outside interest or attendance at the same church/golf club/university alumni reunion. As Goffee and Jones put it:

> Most great leaders have highly developed social antennae: they use a complex mix of cognitive and observational skills to recognise what followers are consciously – and unconsciously – signalling to them.[5]

And this is one of the reasons why successful people often choose their clothes with care. They know what will work best in a particular environment. They know what impact they are trying to have. Are they trying to shock? Are they trying to seem down to earth? Are they trying to look like a maverick? Or do they want to be accepted by their audience? The aim of being political is to have influence and you can only have influence if you are visible. Enabler Sharon Connolly, who helps successful executives get their image right, understands how important it is to be noticed:

> If a person has been passed over for promotion or is not effec-tively leading their team, if someone blends in to the back-ground, they have to get out there, they have to be seen. When people are networking, your effectiveness is 70 per cent down to visibility and only 30 per cent down to ability, so you need to be seen for the right reasons. Whatever you do, you need to tell people about it and that's often why people look at their clothes and make some changes.

This ability to adapt your style and approach in order to connect applies whoever you are trying to influence. Let's say you want to make a connection with Key Holder Oli Barrett. He explained to me that he gets contacted regularly by people who want to meet with him in the hope he can open doors for them. Most requests do not result in a meeting, but if someone has made an effort to find out something about him and work that into the request – 'So did you really run a networking event with the dragons from *Dragons' Den*?' and then perhaps acknowledges, 'I know you are short of time but can I meet with you?' – he is far more likely to create a window in his diary.

The need for political skills is something that Star Maker and headhunter Lucy Harris acknowledges is vital for her candidates:

> I would love to think it is possible to operate at that level and not play politics. But politics usually present themselves at that level because of the complex dynamics and the value of that relationship to the organisation. As Chief Exec of an organisa-tion, you are making decisions that involve complex scenarios and complex strategy. You cannot make decisions without pleasing some people and upsetting other people and that in itself is, to a degree, political. Just being yourself can be a good thing or a bad thing depending on how that person behaves. Sometimes you have to have more of a business etiquette which may mean moulding yourself in order to be a player. That may be an example of playing politics.

But such 'good politics' is different from pure manipulation. It still reflects aspects of the individual's real self. People who are good at this kind of politics know which of their own personality traits to reveal and when. Sometimes, when we experience this kind of 'good poli-tics' in action, we even know that we are being slightly 'managed' but we don't mind because we understand that the world of work plays by slightly different rules anyway.

Whenever we are in a negotiation situation, we recognise that a certain amount of 'bluffing' is acceptable. According to Albert Carr, a former White House adviser to President Truman, this kind of bluffing is very different to lying:

Most executives from time to time are almost compelled, in the interests of their companies or themselves, to practise some form of deception when negotiating . . . By conscious misstatements, concealment of pertinent facts or exaggeration – in short bluffing – they seek to persuade others to agree with them. I think it is fair to say that if the individual executive refuses to bluff from time to time – if he feels obligated to tell the truth, the whole truth, and nothing but the truth – he is ignoring opportunities permitted under the rules and is at a heavy disadvantage in his business dealings.[6]

Well, having worked in the White House, he should know!

Where the line between 'good politics' and 'bad politics' is drawn here, according to Carr, is unique to the individual.

Businesspeople (or anyone in any field) must be able to reconcile themselves to the bluff in which they play a part. They need to make sure they won't lose their self-respect and that their actions are in line with their own standards of honesty, taking into account the requirements of their work. They must feel ethically justified.

Politics can turn bad, though, when a business becomes unsettled by some event and becomes dysfunctional. For instance, when a business is run in a highly structured directive style, frictions can start to develop and people start to rebel. As mentioned earlier, today's workforce don't respond well to being told exactly what to do and how to do it for long periods of time. As there is no way in this environment to bring about change in an open, transparent way because anyone suspected of doing that will be shot down, people can only influence behind closed doors. Factions develop and the rules of the game become skewed.

People regularly disagree with one another in organisations, but this isn't necessarily dangerous. In fact, it is vital for a healthy organisation to give voice to different perspectives. Politics, in this environment, is played in accordance with the rules of business: you adjust your tone and message to your audience and ensure you are expressing authentic parts of yourself at the same time. You believe that what you are trying to achieve is in the best interests of your business (or your team, or society) and you use the rules of business to give you the best chance of getting the result.

In a dysfunctional environment, however, people stop playing by the rules and go underground. And where there is either a highly centralised command and control power system or, just as danger-ous, a power vacuum because of weak management at the top, people are almost encouraged to jockey for position and push others out of their way by whatever means necessary.

Most of us, whether we are very senior, very junior or work for ourselves, want to have some influence over our lives. When we lack power – either because of a dictatorial leadership style or a power vacuum – we become frustrated by our inability to make decisions which directly affect our wellbeing. That's when we feel forced to become 'bad politicians'.[7] Enabler Vicki Day described such a situation from her working life:

> Lots of people don't want to play politics, but even if there are just two of you in the office, one of you might not make a cup of tea for the other one and that can be political. There is always point-scoring. I remember one executive always trying to seem so nice, so ethical, but it was obvious she was a cow and I thought, 'Why don't you just come out and be one? Don't sit there eating mung beans and pretending to be a woolly tree hugger.' I would much rather work with someone who is a pain in the backside – you know how to prepare your-self – instead of someone airy fairy but secretly stabbing you in the back.

CREATING YOUR OWN POLITICAL PARTY

The extent to which you play politics is a judgement call for you personally, as is the style of that politics. Politics can be as simple as being an effective communicator, or it can be as complex as having an intricate knowledge of the motivations and beliefs of those around you and adapting your style continually to bring about the results you want to see. And, of course, some people will enjoy the game itself far more than the results of it, which is when we will start to see behaviour that makes us suspicious. What is certainly true is that you must be *in* the game in order to succeed, whatever field you work in.

POLITICS RECIPE

(Some people prefer a more sour taste, in which case add more common or garden manipulation.)

- Decide what you want to achieve in your role, whether it's the one you play in your business or in society at large.
- Take a bunch of your ethical beliefs and authentic personality and chop up to suit your own taste and the taste of those around you.
- Add emotional awareness so that you clearly understand what motivates and inspires the people you deal with.
- Make sure you mix in a solid track record to gain the trust of others.
- Sprinkle the most palatable mixture over those you want to influence.
- Feel free to adjust the recipe depending on circumstances, as long as this doesn't make it unpleasant for you to eat.

REFERENCES

1 Zaleznik, Abraham. 'Power and Politics in Organisational Life'. *Harvard Business Review*, May/June 1970.

2 Banks, Janet, and Diane Coutu. 'How to Protect Your Job in a Recession'. p.113. *Harvard Business Review*, September 2008.

3 Zaleznik, Abraham. 'Power and Politics in Organisational Life'. *Havard Business Review*, May/June 1970.

4 Goffee, Rob, and Gareth Jones. 'Managing Authenticity: The Paradox of Great Leadership'. p.3. *Harvard Business Review*, December 2005.

5 Goffee, Rob, and Gareth Jones. 'Managing Authenticity: The Paradox of Great Leadership'. p.5. *Harvard Business Review*, December 2005.

6 Carr, Albert Z. 'Is Business Bluffing Ethical?' p.3. *Harvard Business Review*, January/February 1968.

7 Bourgeois III, L.J. Kathleen Eisenhardt, and Jean Kahwajy. 'How Management Teams Can Have a Good Fight'. p.6. *Harvard Business Review*, July/August 1997.

Ingredient 7

Talent

So far, all of the ingredients in the recipe for success have focused on personal qualities – your own or those of the people around you. They have related to personality traits – good manners, having a trust-worthy nature, being able to read other people and adapt your style to meet their needs. But where does actual ability at some tangible skill come in the recipe? Surely you have to be exceptional at some-thing practical, be hugely knowledgeable in some area or have a rare and valued talent which few of your contemporaries share? At least, one might think, you need to be smart.

The answer is not straightforward. There are individuals in many fields who have relied heavily on a talent to propel them to power, but there are also many talented people who struggle for success. Talent alone, even exceptional talent, does not seem to guarantee success. Having said that, without any discernable skill it would also be hard to get to the top. So how much talent is enough? What kinds of talents are most valuable? And can one have too much?

WHAT IS TALENT?

Do you know what your talents are? Are they innate or learnt? Have you always known where your gift lies or did it emerge later in life? Are you still looking for yours? I believe everyone has the potential to excel in a wide variety of areas. We also have weaknesses at skills we find much harder to master. One of the problems with relying on a talent in order to achieve success is that we assume we are only exposed to the opportunity to develop our strengths randomly.

What if no one had ever given Steve Backley a javelin to throw? What if George Best's parents had banned him from playing football because it was distracting him from his schoolwork? Ellen MacArthur only decided to become a professional sailor when a bout of glandular fever got in the way of her sixth form studies and prevented her from becoming a vet. If you weren't given the opportunity to excel at something, you may believe you have a talent of which you are totally unaware. If only someone had given you a javelin, you could have been successful too.

The good news is that innate talent might not exist at all. You might be born with a propensity to be able to learn something with more ease than someone else. But talent is always learnt. We are not born good at anything. 'What about Mozart?' I hear you cry. Yes, he is typically presented as a child prodigy, born with an innate gift, but don't forget that his achievement was only extraordinary in comparison with the general standards of the day. Whether he would stand out now is unknown. Also, he started learning music before he was four years old and his father was a skilled composer and a famous teacher, having written one of the first books on violin instruction. It is less of a surprise that he was so talented than we are led to believe.

All the 100 or more superb performers studied for *The Cambridge Handbook of Expertise and Expert Performance*, including those from fields as diverse as surgery, acting, chess, writing, computer programming, ballet, music, aviation and firefighting, show that expertise is made not born. It is the amount and quality of the practice which influences the level of expertise people achieve rather than any innate gift.[1] Authors K. Anders Ericsson, Michael J. Prietula and Edward T. Cokely have studied the theory of expertise and conclude that it will take the average person at least a decade to achieve it and only then if they focus on 'tasks beyond your current level of competence and comfort'. To get to the very top, the authors argue that: you've got to forget the folklore about genius that makes many people think they cannot take a scientific approach to developing expertise.[2]

In other words, whatever field you are in now, you can excel in terms of your expertise. As long as you have the motivation, the interest and the other qualities already discussed in previous chapters you can develop an exceptional ability . . . if you are willing to put in the time.

Deliberate practice means working particularly on the aspects of your game that you can't do well, or even at all, as well as improving those areas where you have a strength. This is not the same as working in a field which is a bad fit for you. If you have no 'feel' for the majority of what you are required to do, you probably have little interest in investing the time or energy to achieve excellence.

This may sound contradictory – on the one hand there is no such thing as innate skill, on the other there are clearly skills you take to more readily than others, but we all know there are some skills we find easier to learn. Within that overall tendency to be good at something though, there will be aspects that we find more challenging. You might have always felt very comfortable with a golf club in your hands, but that's not a talent in a meaningful way and it won't win you the Ryder Cup. Becoming a masterful player involves more than having a good feel for the game. It involves deliberate practice of every shot, over and over, from the exact same location, in order to experiment with different techniques and hone that skill.

That doesn't mean you need to practise every minute of the day. Most experts, including athletes, writers and musicians, only practise for four or five hours at a time and some for even less time. That is because deliberate practice is mentally demanding. The famous violinist Nathan Milstein wrote:

> Once when I became concerned because others around me practised all day long, I asked [my mentor] Professor Auer how

many hours I should practise, and he said, 'It really doesn't matter how long. If you practise with your fingers, no amount is enough. If you practise with your head, two hours is plenty.[3]

No matter how 'naturally' you take to a particular skill, what really counts is whether you have the ability and commitment to continually improve.

Literary agent Carole Blake takes on authors at different stages in their development:

I have taken on clients when they've written a few chapters and when they've already written a few novels. If I am taking on someone who hasn't finished their novel, I need to believe they can finish it well. I do a lot of moulding because I edit their work, but I want to see that they are learning from that process and that each book needs less editing. The ability to learn from feedback is important, otherwise you won't have a long career.

Those who achieve high levels of expertise learn from a variety of sources. They may start with someone who can give a lot of time and praise (a local teacher or someone you admire in your own department). Then they progress to someone more advanced and eventually to someone who has achieved an exceptional level of success. They need to be able to take on board constructive, honest, even painful, feedback and also, according to K. Anders Ericsson et al, know when a coach's feedback doesn't work for them:

The elite performers we studied knew what they were doing right and concentrated on what they were doing wrong. They deliberately picked unsentimental coaches who would challenge them and drive them to higher levels of performance.

WHAT TALENT IS THE RIGHT TALENT?

As we have seen, it is possible to develop a talent; indeed, it is vital to develop a talent. Relying on your natural feel for something is limiting. However, there still remains the question of what talent it is that you should be developing. The obvious answer would be the core skill of your job. If you want to be finance director, you need to be expert at spreadsheets and budgeting. If you want to be operations director you have to be the best on the shop floor. Right? Not necessarily.

Such skills are great when your job is compiling spreadsheets and operating machinery, but as you progress through your career you may need some of these skills less. In fact, the more skilled you are at these tasks, the more difficulty you may have as you move through your organisation. I have worked with many leaders who have skills in one specific area and have developed those to such an extent that they are reluctant to pass that work on to someone else when they step up to the next level. They keep stepping in and checking spreadsheets, analysing sales data, getting involved in the detail because that's what they always enjoyed and what they were very skilled at. Managing people, taking a visionary perspective, having a light touch when delegating may be more important. But these are skills they have neglected to develop because their focus has been so narrow.

According to mentor, strategist and Enabler John Savage, having too much talent in one area can be limiting:

It is a fine thing to have marvellous ability whether you are a dancer or a musician, or whatever. But it is like having a grand tool which you can't get the best from if you don't know how to use it, unless you've built up an understanding of the other aspects, unless you understand the protocols of working with the tool. I have seen doctors who are fantastically brilliant, but they haven't worked out the other tools so they can be impossibly difficult. Sometimes a beautiful talent can overarch everything, as with George Best. He was quite exceptional as a young man and, although he had his problems, people were very forgiving because of his talent. But for most people, excessive reliance on a particular ability is dodgy. I've seen people hobbled by their ability and they don't seem to have the brain-space to add other bits to it.

Knowing what other bits to add – the talents that matter if you want to become a success – is vital. According to headhunter Lucy Harris, chief executives and managing directors need depth and breadth to be effective:

> The challenge is to be fantastic in a silo and then develop your portfolio to be really good at more than one area. The talent is to multitask, to keep the balls in the air and be charming, relevant, a great communicator, motivate a team, develop the strategy and do all that at once. You are the conductor, even if you have brilliant people around you. And getting to be the conductor is a very broad task.

Having breadth of knowledge applies outside your own business – to your industry and related industries. Without it, you lack credibility. No matter how good a writer you may be, if you don't know about anything you can't write about anything. No matter how great a leader you are, people won't follow you if they don't think you understand what is happening in the wider world.

The ability to absorb information easily and quickly (which is related to the ability to learn from feedback) and then assimilate that information in order to make decisions confidently is a valuable talent. Successful people take action. Leo Tolstoy once observed that people often told him they didn't know whether or not they could write a novel because they had never tried. The first step to success would seem to be taking the first step . . . and then the next and the next. Indecisive people never get off the starting block.

It is something HR professional Phil Taylor wants to see if he is going to open doors for people:

> There is a basic technical competence – being good at what they do – but it is the ability to connect that to a bigger vision, the ability to articulate that and engage others, those that are willing to drive change, those that are willing to try something different, those that are willing to take on a variety of different responsibilities or different challenges . . . Performance is a ticket to play but I also want them to show an aptitude to take on different things, to broaden their scope. When I am looking for talent for senior positions, I want them to have the attitude 'I don't need to see a job description, I will see what needs doing'. So people who can pick up on what the important issues are and then align people around them rather than waiting for someone to tell them this is important . . . That's what I want to see.

Tycoon Peter Jones encourages all would-be entrepreneurs to keep their eyes, and ears, open. Urging them to (in his words) 'commit to learning', he feels that all entrepreneurial people have a natural willingness to seek out new information:

> . . . not academic knowledge but practical knowledge that comes from listening, observing and learning from life itself. If we can open ourselves up to new ideas and new ways of thinking, the world really is our oyster.[4]

Not only does learning enable us to become more expert and more talented, gaining and retaining knowledge enables you to be more creative, generate more original ideas and, consequently, be more forward thinking and a more effective agent of change.

New ideas are produced when two seemingly unrelated concepts collide. Look at the following list of words:

Train	Scissors	Toy	Snow	Tap
President	Toothbrush	Hamburger	Battery	Eagle
Soup	Parachute	Beer	Hospital	Shoe
Snail	Mouse	Cloud	Food Blender	Tax
Bed	Frog	Jazz	Hat	Towel

Pick any word randomly and see if you can think of any new products that relate to this word, e.g. new products that are sparked by the word 'train'. Now pick a second word randomly. What new products can you think of when you bring the two words together, e.g. new products sparked by the words 'train' and 'jazz'?

It was probably easier to think of ideas when you had two words rather than just one. If you knew a lot about trains and jazz, you could be even more original in your thinking. Try the experiment again, but choose two words you know something about (you can pick two words that are not on this list, but try to make sure they are as unrelated to each other as possible).

What makes the difference between the creative person and the less creative person is not any special power but greater knowledge (in the form of practised expertise) and the motivation to acquire it.[5] We come back, again, to the importance of learning and working hard to develop expertise.

One talent that Enabler Vicki Day has observed is the extreme clarity that successful people have when they think and communicate. They are able to sift through all this information, all of these ideas, all of the conflicting messages and pull out the simple, understandable themes and details which make all the difference:

Very successful people are meticulous in the way they communicate. It's all about clean, clear messages and there is no haziness. No one can say 'I wasn't sure about that so I did this' or 'I misinterpreted that and I took this from your e-mail or that from your e-mail.' They may even come across as control freaks and sometimes they are. It is their baby and their vision, so they don't want anyone to muddy the water. It is about attention to detail, drilling down to the last comma. That might go against the current management thinking because it is a form of control, but in everything you do in life you need guidance and guidelines. Say you open a shop and you've got all the stock. You are in the best location and you want to do £1 million in the first year. You don't then just leave it up to the sales staff, you have to give them the tools, show them exactly what they need to do, how to use the stock they have to make a million pounds.

Successful people don't overwhelm you with details, but they know exactly what to tell you and how to tell you so that you get the message clearly. They have pulled together all their years of expertise and transferred it to you to enable you to benefit from all of that experience. It's something that Oli Barrett values as well:

I notice how people communicate. Can they move from the fast flow fire-hose mode, spilling out 100mph, to the more clinical, get things done, less-is-more style? Can they change register? When people get down to work I want them to be diligent and succinct. It is not a common thing.

CHOOSING YOUR TALENT

It is time to choose where you are going to put all your hard work. As we have seen, you can create a 'kitchen cabinet' of advisers and people who have skills in areas which will never be a good fit for you. While breadth is important, you won't be able to develop an expertise in everything, no matter how many hours you practise.

So, you need to decide what is most important to *you* and what is most likely to lead to your success. The to *you* element is very important. In many fields, we see people who excel and yet do not seem to find any pleasure in what they do. Although I said in Chapter 5 that we tend to enjoy doing things we are good at, this enjoyment can be seriously damaged if we are motivated by the need to please other people rather than the desire to achieve for ourselves. And when enjoyment goes, so does motivation.

The ability to learn, retain and apply knowledge, generate ideas and make decisions has already been identified as an important talent in this chapter. You may already exhibit some expertise at one or more of these already. You may believe yourself to have more talent than you actually do. And however accurate your self-assessment, there is always room for improvement.

It is time to get some of that honest, painful feedback. Start by identifying a variety of people from inside and outside work who know you well enough to comment on your strengths. You can conduct informal research, sitting down with a cup of tea and asking them what they notice about you. Alternatively, you can compose an e-mail which will give them more time to think about their answers. Explain that you are looking for honesty and are open to critique because you want to continue to learn. Remember to include as many questions about your strengths as your areas of weakness.

Some sample questions
1. How do I currently add value in my job/in our relationship?
2. When you think of me, what words come to mind?
3. Which areas would be most valuable for me to develop?
4. Which areas should I get others to do or get help with?
5. Can you give examples of when I used my strengths?
6. Can you give examples of when you've seen my weaknesses?
7. Who could help me work on my strengths? And my weaknesses?

Next, look at the feedback for patterns. Don't ignore inconsistencies – some people might have a more astute insight into your strengths and weaknesses or have experienced you under certain conditions which brought out different traits. Equally, you don't have to focus on all the feedback with the same vigour. As we saw earlier in this chapter, part of the skill is knowing which feedback to take on board and which doesn't suit you.

Write a description of yourself based on your insight following this feedback. This piece of prose should include examples given to you by the people who gave you feedback. When you read it back it should sound like you.

Now decide where to do your deliberate practice. Which areas, if you worked on them, would make the biggest impact on your effectiveness? Some of these will already be areas of strength. Others will be more challenging. If there are areas in the feedback where you show no natural ability, think of ways you can minimise the impact of these, for instance getting other people to do them for you.

Not everyone who has picked up a javelin would be able to compete at Olympic level just because they had the best coaches and put in the hours of training. Not everyone can be a world-class orator or best-selling author or decisive leader if they don't have the natural fit. But no one, no matter how naturally they fit with a particular talent, will be a world-class orator or best-selling author or decisive leaders unless they push themselves to achieve expertise.

TALENT RECIPE
- You can whip up a wide range of talents if you are willing to put in time for dedicated practice.
- Being a talented pastry chef may serve you well at the beginning of your career but you will also need a breadth of knowledge in all areas if you are to run the restaurant.

- Over-reliance on an exceptional talent can mean you neglect other tools.
- Despite the fact that talents can be learnt, each of us will find some easier than others to master.
- Talents which matter include the ability to engage other people, to communicate clearly, to assimilate information, to learn, to generate ideas and make decisions.
- Whatever your talent, you must be able to apply it in a real way rather than only having theoretical knowledge. Being able to recite the recipe for a Victoria sponge is not the same as being able to make one.
- Get feedback in order to judge how you are performing and which areas need more work.

REFERENCES

1 Anders Ericsson, Karl, et al. *The Cambridge Handbook of Expertise and Expert Performance*. Cambridge: Cambridge University Press, 2006.
2 Anders Ericsson, Karl, Edward T. Cokely, and Michael J. Prietula. 'The Making of an Expert'. p.116. *Harvard Business Review*, July/August 2007.
3 Anders Ericsson, Karl, Edward T. Cokely, and Michael J. Prietula. 'The Making of an Expert'. p.119. *Harvard Business Review*, July/August 2007.
4 Jones, Peter. *Tycoon*. p.250. London: Hodder & Stoughton, 2007.
5 Boden, Margaret. *The Creative Mind*. p.24. 4th ed. London: Abacus, 1996.

Ingredient 8

Insatiable Appetite

The question remains, why do successful people feel the need to achieve? We have seen how committed they are, how focused, how sturdy they are when under attack. We've seen how they gather around them a close army of allies and how they build trust on a wider basis in order to bring about the changes they believe are vital. We've seen how hard they work to build up their knowledge and expertise. But why? What drives them?

A US study of Olympic athletes carried out just before the 2000 Sydney Games showed that 52 per cent of athletes would take a drug that would make them unbeatable for the next five years, even if it was then guaranteed to kill them.[1] That's a pretty high level of commitment to winning.

Most successful people have made choices which, to the rest of us, seem like sacrifices. They may have compromised on time with their family or, perhaps, chosen not to have a family at all in order to pursue their career goals. They may have struggled financially for many years while their peers worked in steady jobs with comfortable incomes. Actress Liz Smith, best known for her roles in *The Vicar of Dibley* and *The Royle Family*, held down two or three jobs at a time as she raised her children alone while still trying to break into acting. It wasn't until she was in her 50s that she had more than a walk-on part in any television show. Only then did her dreams of acting as a career take off. Many of us would have thrown in the towel decades earlier.

According to Professor Graham Jones and former Olympic swimmer Adrian Moorhouse, people are capable of extraordinary commitment when they take the attitude that they have chosen to do a particular thing rather than feeling they have been forced. They believe their motivation is healthy because they can rationalise it. It doesn't feel like a sacrifice to fly from New York to London for a meeting and then return to New York that evening to attend another important meeting in the morning if they believe that they have chosen to do it because it serves a greater good.

What you consider to be a 'greater good' is personal to you. People are motivated by a variety of factors. Just as we all like our steak cooked in a slightly different way, we all get motivated by a slightly different combination of factors, but when you find the right combination of motivations for you, and find work which allows you to indulge this personal taste, you can achieve great results.

THEORIES OF MOTIVATION

There are many theories about what motivates us and what demotivates us, but we'll look in more detail at the work of the granddaddy of motivation theory, Frederick Herzberg.

Herzberg found through his research that the things that make us dissatisfied in our work do not make us more motivated when they are reversed. The opposite of job dissatisfaction is not job satisfaction. Someone who complains about the food in the canteen doesn't suddenly become highly engaged with their work when the food is improved, and the same applies to pay. We may complain about the size of our pay packet and blame that for our lazy attitude, but when we are paid more, the evidence shows that improvements in our motivation are short-lived. The way to motivate a poorly performing member of staff is not to threaten them with a pay cut or loss of benefits, but to tickle their taste buds with the chance to get their innate motivations met.[2]

Herzberg says that 'push and pull' motivation (tempting people with a carrot while prodding them with a stick) doesn't work with most people for long. It is fine when you are trying to get your dog off the sofa; you give him a nudge from behind or offer him a treat if he will comply and you end up with an obedient pet. But people are more complicated than that. We might think that a pay rise or more time off will give us more job satisfaction, but it doesn't. It simply reduces job dissatisfaction. True satisfaction must come from within.

Herzberg's study, followed by numerous others which tried to test his theories further, concluded that there were six innate motivators which, when present in our work, enrich our employment and make it meaningful for us. They are:

1. **Achievement.** This need, when met, has the most motivating affect on performance. It seems that most of us get a kick out of achieving goals and when we do, we want to set even more challenging and stretching ones. Success based on your ability, expertise, experience and skills (which is totally under your control) gives you a sense of pride. Pride feeds your self-esteem. You feel good about yourself which makes you want to work even harder to get more of this feeling.[3]
2. **Recognition.** This is different from a pat on the back. It means your achievement being noticed in a meaningful way for you by someone whose recognition is valued by you. This will be different for different people. Many of us do not want an awards ceremony where we are presented with a certificate by the company chairman in front of tipsy colleagues. Instead, a one-to-one with our boss who explains exactly what she has seen us do and how impressed she is might have more meaning. On the other hand, winning a gold medal in front of the world's media and standing on the podium while they play the national

anthem does it for many athletes. And there is nothing wrong
with that.

3. **The work itself.** A great deal of motivation comes from
enjoying what you do and this should be no surprise. However,
there are many people who wonder why they aren't getting
ahead when they clearly don't enjoy what they do. Perhaps
the job has not lived up to their expectations. Many of us know
very little about our profession before we embark on it.
We may spend many years training to do a job only to find
that we don't enjoy it once we get the opportunity to do it for
real. I loved my early years in broadcasting, but eventually felt
that 90 per cent of my day was taken up with activities which
I didn't enjoy. At that point, my career had stagnated. What a
surprise. Although, as a Radio 4 producer I held a much
coveted job, I did not feel successful because I was not enjoying
my work.

It can be hard to admit that, after all that studying, all that
grafting, all that dreaming, your work isn't what you expected it
to be and you are going to make a change. Many people put off
that decision, waiting for fate to step in and force them to
change. This happens occasionally when people are made
redundant. They finally get the opportunity to fund their true
ambition and it takes off. Because they love it they don't feel it is
work and therefore they are happy to do it in the evening, at the
weekend and on holiday, much to the dismay of their other half I
am sure. If you want to be successful, make sure you are doing
something you like.

4. **Responsibility.** This is a controversial one. All the research
shows that when people's jobs are 'enlarged' – they are given
more to do without more pay or status – motivation levels drop
and continue to fall. However, when jobs are 'enriched' and
people are given more responsibility and ownership, motivation
levels – after an initial fall – will rise and continue to do so. The

initial fall is interesting and, it is thought, occurs because people don't understand that they will feel more motivated if they have more responsibility. They rebel or feel overwhelmed at first, but as time goes on they begin to feel energised.[4]

If you plan on being a success, you need to not only accept more responsibility when it is offered, but seek more responsibility. Your competition won't come only from colleagues in your own company or even in other companies in the country: in today's international market, it could be coming from elsewhere in the world such as Asia and Latin America where people are more forthright about asking for more responsibility.

5. **Advancement.** People respond well to the feeling that they are moving forward in life. Staying still can feel as negative as being given a pay cut or being demoted. When we have opportunities to advance in our career, we have something to strive for. This may be why many of the top businesspeople I have worked with begin to look for new challenges once they reach the top (or once the top is in sight). After a lifetime of pushing themselves up the ladder, they don't feel ready to stop. They will either look outside their work for new challenges or invent new milestones in their role. As Jones and Moorhouse put it, those who have achieved a long-held ambition:

> may begin to question the meaning of life and actually become quite unhappy because they perceive themselves to have no direction any more. Others deal with this situation in a much more constructive manner by 'transferring' their motivation to other things.[5]

6. **Growth.** As with advancement, people want to feel they are growing and learning. We saw what the rewards for developing a talent can be and many people find this whole process of developing themselves highly motivational. When our work

challenges and stretches us, teaching us new things about ourselves and about our area of expertise, we feel more accomplished. Those who find this most motivational will be happiest in roles where learning is a key aspect of the job. Researchers, academics and scientists may all enjoy their work because it focuses on learning. For the rest of us, learning is a by-product of the role but one which adds to the meaningfulness of our job.

AND THEN SOME . . .

Successful people are motivated. They care, like the rest of us, about achieving goals and getting recognition for those achievements. They have found work which they enjoy and have taken on more and more responsibility, rising up the ranks as they do so, and they have continued to grow and seek out opportunities to learn.

No big surprise there. But it is more than that. They have an insatiable appetite. There is no such thing as 'enough' for them. They are never finished. Unlike many of us, they don't dream of retirement (except perhaps on the odd bad day). They never want to stop achieving, growing, getting recognition, advancing . . . whatever it is that keeps them going. It's as if they have an itch that never feels fully scratched, or a stomach that never feels full. And that may be why, if you ask them whether they are successful, they rarely answer 'yes'.

The reason why these people are never quite finished and therefore are always pushing themselves to achieve more, is that their definition of success is set at an extremely high level. In effect, they cannot actually achieve it so they remain hungry. Take Key Holder Phil Taylor. He is responsible for human resources at Mattel around the world (excluding, as he pointed out, the US), but describes himself as 'moderately successful':

I'm not finished yet. If you had asked me ten years ago whether I would consider myself successful if I was in the role

I am in now, I probably would have said yes. But it is a constantly moving goalpost. You go through phases in your life and you redefine what you want to do. It is pretty smart to take your life experience, knowledge and skill and say I understand better how to employ these, what the possibilities are for me, so I will change my target.

Very successful people keep changing their ultimate goal, moving it further out of reach. This is true for Enabler John Savage. He didn't set out to be a success for himself but in order to bring about social change. He has paid a price for this commitment. His is a hard goal to live with because, until social justice is achieved, he has not succeeded:

I think there is a danger in putting all your energy in to one aspect of life. My obsession with working took me away from my family. There is a sacrificial bit in this, but I believe there is a duty, an obligation, to use whatever talent or ability you've got. That obligation might be to provide money for your family, but I think if you can do more, there is an obligation to serve the common good. Most people don't seek out the things that give their life meaning and satisfaction. When you find something that gives your life meaning, then you are happy. Having said that, I think it is hard to be complacently happy when, in the world, there are over a billion people who are going to starve to death, when there are adults in this country who can't read. I cannot understand why this doesn't influence everybody. I'm only glad I've had the chance to be one of the cogs.

For John, there is never an end to his mission. He keeps going, trying to scratch the itch while knowing it can never be done . . . at least, not in his lifetime.

Star Maker Lucy Harris has a broad definition of success, meaning that she must be spinning a number of plates in the air at all times in order to count herself as successful:

> Success means reaching the top of your game which then fuels your motivation to go further. Each of us is motivated by different things but we all ask ourselves, 'Is what I am achieving enough to supply my motivational demands?' For me, family is very important, so if I am not doing my bit at home with my friends and family as well as professionally, I am failing.

Those of us who are satisfied to set a goal, reach it and say 'I am done' will not achieve exceptional success. 'A man's reach should exceed his grasp or what's a heaven for?' wrote Robert Browning and it seems that, on reaching heaven, these people just want to reach even further. Heaven isn't far enough.

Actually we all need our goals to be slightly out of reach in order to achieve anything. A friend who ran in the London Marathon told me that she was training to run 27 miles rather than 26 miles and 386 yards. She was aiming *beyond* the finish line in order to achieve the necessary distance. In business, if you aim for a £1 million turnover, you are likely to achieve only £500,000. Aim for £2 million and you will be more likely to achieve £1 million. However, this also means £1 million won't feel like enough. And so it is true of successful people.

EXTERNAL PRESSURE

The pressure to continue to succeed doesn't only come from within: there can be external pressures too. Many successful people have lifestyles which need to be sustained; their husbands, wives, children or friends have come to expect a certain quality of life. Deciding to opt out or even scale down can be very unpopular with your nearest and dearest.

Other people's well-being is tied up in your success. When you employ large numbers of people or other people's businesses rely on trade with you, you have a great deal of responsibility. It is something that agent Carole Blake recognises as adding a lot of pressure to her authors:

> There are many authors who really think that once they have published a book it should be easy after that. It isn't. The second book is a nightmare to write and publish because everyone's expectations are higher. It doesn't get easier, it gets harder. Novelist Peter James got reviews for three successive books, each review saying the book was better than the one before, so the expectation on him for the next book is huge. He still has to go back into a quiet room and write that next one. Anyone who says, 'I've got it made now and I can do whatever I want' has got it totally wrong. In writing, you can write two bad books but after that your audience will melt away. I represent career writers and, when I take someone on, I ask them what they plan to do in the future. Are they planning to write more novels? My business is a business too. I need new projects constantly.

The need to please or support others can have a detrimental effect on one's health, even if it is highly motivating for some individuals.

Professor Graham Jones says our behaviour can either be described as 'Approach', where we move towards some set of circumstances, or 'Avoidance', where we avoid or move away from a set of circumstances:[6]

> People who are approach motivated may say, 'It is time to move on, so I've decided to look for another job.' . . . Those executives who are driven by avoidance motives, on the other hand, often refer to being worn down by frustrations in their

current role, the people they work with or perhaps the lack of vision in the organisation . . . These are not the best motives for leaving. . .

'Avoidance' motivation can be seen when people embark on careers in order to please their families. Many doctors, lawyers and accountants were led in to their profession because it was considered high status, secure and lucrative by parents. Their hearts might have been in the right place – 'We want our boy/girl to live in a nice house, have a nice car and have a safe, secure profession' – but, as we have seen, such external factors have far less impact on motivation than internal ones like actually enjoying the work.

A common 'avoidance' motive is fear of failure. It may sometimes result in incredible performances, but there is a high price to pay in terms of personal satisfaction. People motivated by fear of failure always feel they have something to prove, a wrong to right from the past and, even with a proven track record of success, find that their need not to fail is still so strong that they never feel truly satisfied and able to enjoy their success. It is a quality that PA and company managing director Deborah Meredith has found in some of the businesses she has worked with:

Fear of failure might be part of their motivation. The last thing they want to do is fall off the perch. Once they've reached a certain level they have to maintain that level. They have a desire to achieve, they are constantly testing themselves so they have to keep on achieving, pushing the boundaries constantly. It becomes a challenge to stay on top.

'Avoidance' motivation is often found amongst successful people who started with nothing. Many of our best known entrepreneurs, sportspeople, artists and musicians came from the wrong side of the tracks. Their desire to get out of poverty, and bring their family with them, was a powerful force. Vicki Day has noticed that many successful people are motivated towards riches and glory, but also away from their backgrounds:

> The *Sunday Times* Rich List looked at the backgrounds of these successful people and found that many were left as the main breadwinner and had to make money to support their family. I was a single mum for a long time. I was driven because I had to be. Jimmy Tarbuck promised to buy his parents a house before he bought himself one. They want to see all their family do well. They need to nurture and make other people feel secure.

Perhaps success, as you or I define it, doesn't always lie on particularly 'healthy' foundations. As onlookers, we aspire to the level of people we admire, believing that when we get there we will feel 'full'. In truth, the journey towards success never really ends. The goalposts keep moving (we move them), and the needs that drive us never go away. And maybe that's how we like it. It is the journey towards success that gives us energy and motivation, not just achieving the goal. As Winston Churchill said, 'Every day you may make progress. Every step may be fruitful. Yet there will stretch out before you an ever-lengthening, ever-ascending, ever-improving path. You know you will never get to the end of the journey. But this, so far from discouraging, only adds to the joy and glory of the climb.'

INSATIABLE APPETITE RECIPE
- Make choices rather than sacrifices.
- Ask yourself what your innate motivators are, whether you care about achievement, recognition, the work itself, advancement, responsibility or personal growth. Make sure you add your personal needs to your recipe.

- Set goals which are realistic but also beyond easy reach.
- Continue to sprinkle new goals in to your mix as you go so that you are never completely satisfied.
- If necessary, add some 'avoidance' motives to keep you on your toes, but aim for most of your motivation to be 'approach' motivation, in order to sustain your energy for the long haul.
- Enjoy the climb because, chances are, you will never quite reach the peak.

REFERENCES

1 Bond, David. 'A Battle Won, An Unwinnable War'. p.2.14 *The Sunday Times*, 26 October 2003. [Quoted in *Developing Mental Toughness: Gold Medal Strategies for Transforming Your Business Performance* by Professor Graham Jones and Adrian Moorhouse. p.15. Oxford: Spring Hill, 2007.]

2 Herzberg, Frederick. 'One More Time: How Do You Motivate Employees?' *Harvard Business Review*, January 2003. Original published in *Harvard Business Review*, Jan/Feb 1968.

3 Jones, Graham, and Adrian Moorhouse. *Developing Mental Toughness: Gold Medal Strategies for Transforming Your Business Performance.* p.86. Oxford: Spring Hill, 2007.

4 Herzberg, Frederick. 'One More Time: How Do You Motivate Employees?' p.12. *Harvard Business Review*, January 2003.

5 Jones, Graham, and Adrian Moorhouse. *Developing Mental Toughness: Gold Medal Strategies for Transforming Your Business Performance.* p.111. Oxford: Spring Hill, 2007.

6 Jones, Graham, and Adrian Moorhouse. *Developing Mental Toughness: Gold Medal Strategies for Transforming Your Business Performance.* p.112. Oxford: Spring Hill, 2007.

Ingredient 9

Invention

Successful people don't believe in standing still. They haven't got to where they are today by following everyone else's lead. Instead they have brought about change, challenged the status quo, taken products or services further than ever before or simply been faster, better or more efficient. In order to do this, they must be able to imagine. They see not only what 'is', but what 'could be'.

Invention is made up of three parts: creativity, risk tolerance and rule-breaking. It is like a home-made mayonnaise: when it is made correctly, all the ingredients blend together perfectly and become one. There's something apparently magical about it.

Creativity is most commonly associated with the arts – painting, poetry, music, drama – but creative thinking can be found in any industry and any walk of life. Every time you solve a problem in a new way, you are being creative. Creativity can mean inventing new products, but being creative in your thinking can be applied much more broadly. You can be creative in the way you resolve a dispute between two employees. You can be creative in the way you organise your team. You can be creative in the way you generate funding for a project or in the way you achieve your goal without funding.

Creativity is about approaching situations with a fresh eye and having ideas about how to address them. But as an ingredient, invention isn't just about being creative, it is also about taking risks.

Risk-taking is integral to 'invention'. Because invention is inevitably about doing something new or different, there is always the risk it won't work. In some companies, the culture is 'By all means take risks, just as long as they pay off'. In truly inventive environments, the people at the top understand that risks don't always pay. There must be a good chance that they will work – they should not be doomed to failure – but if success is completely assured, it probably isn't a new idea. Success can only be assured once an approach has been tried and tested, refined and repeated, which means success with something new is never guaranteed.

However, most organisations are not risk-tolerant; they want guarantees. And that can be challenging for people who see opportunities for making things better. Without the ability to envision something different, new, more efficient or more profitable, one cannot get ahead. But the path is often blocked by people who will only back a sure thing.

Once you have creativity and risk-tolerance, you then slowly stir in rule-breaking and rule-making. Invention inevitably means changing the rules. Working within the rules or norms of an industry or organisation can limit your options, but changing them opens up a new world of possibilities.

That is not to say that successful people take risks, change the rules and create new solutions just for the fun of it. They don't make changes for change's sake, but they do understand that change is inevitable. The key to successful change is anticipating what is needed and being prepared so that you remain the leading individual, or company, in the future. What makes invention such a tricky ingredient to get right is that it looks from the outside like something magical, a kind of Midas touch that you either have or you don't have. In fact, just like all the ingredients so far, it can be learnt or acquired and is far more about hard graft than being a natural born superhero.

WHAT IS HAPPENING NOW?

The future is not an inevitability which we are expected to second-guess. Really useful creative ideas aren't thought up out of thin air. When people try to imagine the future without any reference to the needs of today, they end up with solutions to problems that don't exist. The reason we aren't wearing gold lamé catsuits and eating cubes of artificially simulated food as imagined by B-list 1960s science-fiction writers is because there is no need. Such ideas seem futuristic rather than realistic because they have no connection with the real demands of the world's population.

The question successful people are always asking isn't 'How would we like things to be?' but 'How are things now?' Jerry Hirshberg, who in the late 1970s created Nissan Design International (now Nissan Design America), one of the most innovative car design labs in the world, calls this kind of thinking 'presenthought'. In his excellent book, *The Creative Priority*, he wrote: '[We] give form to the future based on an imaginative grasp of the potential latent in the current moment.'[1]

Successful people are always looking at what is happening in the world as it affects them and their business right now. They aren't dreamers; they base their decisions about the future on what they see happening today. They extrapolate from that what may happen around the corner and prepare for that. When highly creative chef Heston Blumenthal invents a new dish, he doesn't throw disconnected ingredients in a pan and tell us, 'That's new!' Instead, he looks at what we already eat and then asks what happens if he changes this element or removes that. He starts with 'now'.

Creativity comes from looking at real problems today and trying to solve them. The solutions may come from within an industry, from past experience or from seemingly unrelated sources. Key Holder Phil Taylor believes this kind of thinking is vital to succeed in the corporate world:

You can't predict the future precisely, but you do have an understanding of what's happening in the world and the environment that affects what you are doing. Successful people have an understanding of the world they play in and how different elements can affect what they are trying to achieve. If you don't take in a range of perspectives, you can become blinkered. Those that keep an eye on what is happening in the world are more likely to come out with initiatives and thoughts that drive better results.

When you team the word 'train' with the word 'jazz', you might get 100 ideas, but which ones have worth? Which ones could change the world? Which ones could make money? Only those which meet a current need or solve a current problem (or solve a problem which may be anticipated given the current reality) have the potential to survive. And the broader your perspective, the more likely you are to know what problems are out there and have access to a wide range of stimuli to generate new ideas.

MORE THAN A FEELING

In Chapter 7, we saw briefly how learning and knowledge assist in creativity. When two seemingly unrelated concepts collide, a new idea can be born. The difference between the genius and the crank is that the genius has the knowledge and the expertise to know the difference between the good ideas that emerge and those which don't hold water.

But expertise has a part to play, not only in judging the idea's worth, but forming the idea in the first place. Many inventive people describe the moment of creativity as being sudden, almost magical. They get an idea seemingly from nowhere. Pablo Picasso told a friend, 'I don't know in advance what I am going to put on canvas any more than I decide beforehand what colours I am going to use . . . Each time I undertake to paint a picture I have a sensation of leaping into space. I never know whether I shall fall on my feet. It is only later that I begin to estimate more exactly the effect of my work.'[2]

Latin American novelist Isabel Allende described a similar sensation: 'Somehow inside me – I can say this after having written five books – I know that I know where I am going. I know that I know the end of the book even though I don't know it. It's so difficult to explain.'[3]

And it isn't just artists who describe this feeling. Albert Einstein also described feeling that sensation that he was on the right lines even if he couldn't justify it mathematically, yet. Inventor and science fiction writer Arthur C. Clarke asked the questions: 'Intuition or mathematics? Do we use models to help us find the truth? Or do we know the truth first, and then develop the mathematics to explain it?'[4]

The accounts of those creative people above imply that they come up with the answer to a question or a solution to a problem without actively thinking it through; it just occurs to them. There was no planning involved, no preparatory work, just a flash of inspiration which they were able to assess only later. And this ability to generate ideas and solutions, seemingly out of nowhere, is something many of our experts mentioned as setting certain individuals apart. It may involve an element of trust in oneself, which means that successful people have such strength of conviction that they manifest their ideas . . . whether they are any good or not. As we saw in Chapter 3, the expectancy effect may mean that these people's ideas are no better than anyone else's, they simply believe themselves to be right and push so hard that, eventually, everyone else comes to believe they are right too.

However, there is evidence that this gut feeling is genuinely more often right than not and, even if it is wrong a percentage of the time, trusting it is just as reliable as trusting thorough research and data (because even thorough research and data can be misleading). Enabler John Savage uses his own 'gut feel' to great effect:

Whatever it is that makes you have that feeling, which is real, when I collect data it almost always tells me that what I thought, what I believed, was right. It sounds so cocky to say that, but generally I am right. It gets up people's noses to be right all the time.

Despite their own account of this magical sensation of being right, what looks like 'gut feel' to many successful people, and to us as onlookers, may actually be expertise in disguise.

In reality, before the eureka moment comes a great deal of preparatory work. The person may have tried to solve this specific problem before, using more conventional methods, but not been successful. They might have seen other people try to solve it without success or they may have seen a similar problem in an unrelated industry solved effectively, but not seen the connection with their own issue. They may have spent years working in a particular field gaining a solid grounding which can then be applied to solving a problem later on. They may have developed a set of values borne out of a lifetime of experience which inform their decisions so that, although their decisions seem to be based on nothing but their gut, they are actually based on years of education in the school of life.

Between this preparatory stage and the seemingly sudden 'a-ha' moment, comes a phase of incubation, which can take only a few minutes or last for years, where ideas are generated unconsciously. Many inventive people have reported a sudden illumination after waking up from a nap. Coleridge explained that his poem 'Kubla Khan' came to him in a dream. However, just before falling asleep he had been reading this sentence 'In Xamdu did Cublai Can build a stately Palace'. Not so different from the sentence he scribbled down when he awoke:

In Xanadu did Kubla Khan
    A Stately pleasure-dome decree.[5]

This 'break-out' moment is very common. You will probably report yourself that you get your best ideas in the shower, when walking the dog or in the middle of the night. When we stop trying to consciously think about the idea, the brain does the work for us subconsciously.

This is why many successful people insist on 'thinking time'. They may not come to work every day and sit at their desk staring at a computer screen. Instead, they may find their best ideas occur at the golf course. They may take long lunches with colleagues in order to spark interesting conversations and challenge each other's opinions. At Nissan Design America, staff may go to the cinema during the working day in order to refresh their minds and, perhaps, trigger a break-out moment. Although it can seem like the idea came from nowhere, the ground work has been done some time before.

In addition, successful people aren't complacent about creativity. They put themselves into situations where ideas are most likely to strike. Incubation of an idea can occur when you are doing productive mental work on some other project or piece of work. It doesn't just occur when you are chilling out at the day spa.

Literary agent Carole Blake says creativity is vital for her authors, but that doesn't mean they are unprofessional in their approach to their work. They still do their research and are experts in their field, just as aware of what their competitors are doing as any successful businessperson would be:

> Someone said, 'I always wait for my muse to strike. And I make sure my muse strikes at nine in the morning every day.' Writing is a job and you must treat it like one. Most top writers are aware of what their competitors are doing because they want to make sure they aren't replicating a plot that has just been used. It would be foolish to try to be successful and take no notice of the competition. On the other hand, you can't write all the time looking over your shoulder.

After the creative leap has occurred (whether triggered by the latest blockbuster movie or a late night working on your sales figures), there comes a period of verification where the inventor checks his or her conclusions. It is rare for someone successful to rely solely on their belief in an idea without checking and double-checking their conclusions. For some people, this might mean looking at the data to check that their 'gut feel' was indeed accurate; for others it means refining the work. For others, still, it means getting buy-in from other people. While invention might feel somehow 'magical', it is, in fact, based on quite detailed preparation and then verification. How you choose to present this process is a different matter.

Politically, it might be best to present your conclusions as being based purely on thorough research. That you had the idea in the powder room may be irrelevant or even off-putting. In other environments, there might be more gravitas in presenting your conclusions as being based on your remarkable intuitive abilities. Some organisational cultures want to believe that their leaders possess superpowers which cannot be learnt or replicated. In fact, only you and I know that it was really a combination of hard work, study, experience and knowledge, followed by a nap, a bath or a long walk in the park followed by more hard work and analysis which resulted in the breakthrough idea.

RISK-TAKING – THE DANGERS

The original troubleshooter, the late Sir John Harvey-Jones, told a story about when he was relatively junior at ICI and being sent off to negotiate a rather large £10 million contract. He realised during the negotiations that he might be able to get a better deal for his company and held out for another £200,000. It was a risk, but he figured that if the risk paid off, the extra would go straight down to the bottom line as profit and was sure it was worth pushing for more money. After a few days, he began to get anguished telegrams telling him to conclude the deal and come home. But he was still convinced he could do a better deal. At the last minute, as he was leaving the country, he closed the contract.

On returning to base expecting a hero's welcome, he was remonstrated for putting the business at risk. Harvey-Jones believed that, not only should he have been congratulated but that he should have been praised even if the deal had fallen through. He showed he was willing to take risks for the good of the company and this was a quality which should have been rewarded and encouraged.[6]

What Harvey-Jones experienced will be familiar to most of us who have worked in the corporate environment. It is highly risk-intolerant. This has a number of implications for risk-takers:

1. You may only be able to take small, calculated risks and even then, only when you have an established record of trustworthiness.
2. You may not be able to appear too risk-happy. You may have to act as if you are as cautious as the rest until you are established.
3. You may do as John Harvey-Jones did and stand for what you believe is right, even though it may be unpopular. You will have to judge whether such behaviour marks you out as a future trouble-shooter or as a trouble-maker.
4. Risk-takers are valuable in such an environment (whether companies want to acknowledge that or not) and you could stand out from the crowd exactly because the culture is risk-averse. If you take risks wisely it could be a real USP.

Rule-breaking is also risky when it comes to what you wear. We can all think of examples like Richard Branson or Bill Gates to explain why we can go to work dressed in ripped jeans and ill-fitting jumpers. But the truth is that most people are conservative and have expectations about what successful people will wear. It's something image consultant Sharon Connolly has grappled with. She wants people to feel individual but also knows that, until you make it, you need to dress appropriately for your industry and your company:

> We need to think about first impressions. When you meet a client, it is important to make the right impression. Fifty-five per cent of what you think of a person when you first meet them is based on what they are wearing; 38 per cent will be their manner and 7 per cent will be the content.
>
> Of those who are already at the top, they have got where they are going because they have already earned respect. If I am known in my organisation and I have consistently proven myself to you it doesn't matter what I wear. But the rest of us need some help.

The same analysis should be taken about what to wear as when taking any risk. What is the environment? Does breaking the rules set me apart as a future talent or call into question my professionalism? Will people have more respect for me if I dress unconventionally or less? And how much do I care?

BENDING, BREAKING AND INVENTING THE RULES

Successful people are not satisfied with the status quo. They don't want to tread water, they want to move forward. And moving forward means making changes. As John Harvey-Jones said, 'Unless a company is progressing the whole time, it is, in fact, moving backwards.'[7]

What successful people are able to do is predict what conventions are the right ones to be questioned and which should be left alone. They may decide to dress in a conventional way, but question the rules about how the company is structured. It depends what they believe is most important to challenge.

Just as creativity always uses the current reality as its starting point, change uses current needs as its starting point. Successful people ask, 'What needs to be changed? And what should remain the same? What is working today? And what isn't?' They are not inhibited in their imaginations by today's norms, by the rules, but ask 'How could it be better?'.

At one time, it was hard to imagine paying more than £1.50 for a cup of coffee. Today, thanks to Howard Schultz and his Starbucks chain, people regularly pay over £3 for a hot drink. People probably told Schultz that there was no appetite for such expensive coffee. What is so special about one type of coffee that ordinary people, not connoisseur coffee drinkers, would shell out nearly a fiver to sit on a squishy sofa and drink flavoured milk foam? But they do. Schultz didn't let the norms of his day stand in the way of his thinking.

The same applies to Virgin Atlantic Airways. Richard Branson was told by Freddie Laker that an airline was the easiest (and probably most fun) way to lose millions of dollars. Despite the fact that he had to compete with world-class players who had been in the market decades longer, Branson went ahead and created one of the most profitable businesses in his empire. He didn't let 'the rules' stand in his way.

But rules should only be broken when you have something better to put in their place. A company which changes its brand in order to appeal to a younger market, but doesn't consider that its current customers will be alienated by this change, suffers as a result of change. A company which can broaden its appeal while still valuing its current customer base makes a change for the better. The same is true in any field. Star Maker Carole Blake, who represents some of the top fiction writers in the UK, says that successful authors must always balance the need to be inventive with the need to please their readers:

Once an author becomes successful, they have a much better choice of what to write and how to write. Ken Follett has changed direction many times because his audience is so big they will follow him. But if you are writing in a genre that has its own rules in that the audience has an expectation of certain things, if you start straying from the expectations of your audience, they will leave you. Also the market, retailers and publishers want commercial authors to deliver a book a year. Otherwise staff turnover in bookshops means a buyer hasn't heard of them if they haven't written for two years. The market expects continuity. Peter James delivers his book at the beginning of August every year and it always goes straight in to the bestseller list when it's published the next June. Consumers and book store buyers have come to expect a new summer bestseller from him.

Key Holder Oli Barrett agrees:

It is easy to break the rules. It is less easy to come up with a replicable way of doing it. I don't just decide to take Monday morning off to just lie in bed. That would be breaking the rules, but what is the point in that? But if I say I take one day off a week to think and come up with new ideas, that's a new rule that can also influence and inspire others to do the same. If there is a genuinely more effective way to do something, then you can explain it to other people and influence them to change the way they do things too. There must be method in your madness.

Rule-breaking may look radical, but successful rule-breaking is always a balancing act. Not only do customers resist any kind of change, but employees are also uncomfortable with change. People are habitual – just look at the food you eat every week. How often do you try something completely new? We are so resistant to change that organisations which bring about structural change, even if no job losses are made, often find that productivity reduces initially before exceeding previous performance levels once things have settled down. People simply dig in their heels at first.

At certain times in the economic cycle, people with more tolerance for rule-breaking and change will do very well. Lucy Harris, who specialises in headhunting for the retail sector, says that the current economic slump will be good for some of her candidates:

> Those people who are hungry for challenge and volatility will do really well this year because there is something to get on with. They are change merchants. Not all of them enjoy a sustainable environment and they recognise that.

At other times, those of us who like to shake things up will be less in demand and sometimes a more steady hand is needed. Even then, though, change is inevitable. The difference is only how radical that change is and how the message is communicated to a sensitive and less robust audience.

Having the invention ingredient is as much about communication as it is about having original ideas. You have to judge what your audience wants of you. Do they want you to appear radical or steady? Do they want you to have supernatural powers or be down to earth? Do they want you to surprise them or hold their hand? Successful people are able to bring about great changes without losing the support they require. They may, of course, put off some people (some readers, some employees, some voters, some fans) when they change direction, broaden their appeal or introduce a new product. But they have managed the message in such a way that the people they count on come with them.

And that's the magical bit about invention.

INVENTION RECIPE

- Invention is like a sauce made from creativity, risk and rule-breaking.
- Creativity is most commonly found where expertise and preparation are left to stew for some time. This can seem to be a magical process but, in truth, can be carried out by anyone.
- Once the mixture has stewed and a new idea has been produced, it normally needs to be worked into something usable and backed up with facts.
- Most environments are hostile to change and risk, which means you must either appear to be more cautious or take risks openly and live with the consequences.
- Inventiveness can be used to address any challenge or problem. However, it should be applied to current day or realistic future issues if the results are to be of value.
- Use your emotional intelligence to judge how to communicate messages about change. People have more of an appetite at some times than at others.

REFERENCES

1 Hirshberg, Jerry. *The Creative Priority: Driving Innovative Business in the Real World*. p.201. New York: HarperBusiness, 1998.
2 Root-Bernstein, Robert S. and Michele Root-Bernstein. *Sparks of Genius: The Thirteen Thinking Tools of the World's Most Creative People*. p.2. Boston: Mariner Books, 2001.
3 Ibid.
4 Root-Bernstein, Robert S. and Michele Root-Bernstein. *Sparks of Genius: The Thirteen Thinking Tools of the World's Most Creative People*. p.5. Boston: Mariner Books, 2001.
5 Ibid.
6 Boden, Margaret. *The Creative Mind*, p.18. London: Abacus 1992.
7 Harvey-Jones, John. *Making It Happen: Reflections on Leadership*. p.88. London: Fontana/Collins, 1988.
8 Harvey-Jones, John. *Making It Happen: Reflections on Leadership*. p.23. London: Fontana/Collins, 1988.

Ingredient 10

Graft

Developing or honing the qualities already discussed in this book is going to take time and energy. No one is born a success. All successes are created, primarily by the individual themselves. The best restaurants don't buy their chicken Kievs ready-made and frozen for convenience; they lovingly put all the ingredients together in a hot, sweaty kitchen, starting early in the morning and leaving late at night. It takes work.

Some people certainly have more opportunity to achieve success – those whose mother or father owns the business, those with a hefty inheritance to support themselves while they work at their craft, those with supportive families and friends. But, as we have already seen, many people become successful despite hardship and limited life chances. They find a way. And, even if the potential to succeed is handed to you on a plate, it is easy to throw it all away. Complacency, laziness or bad judgement can turn a silk purse into a sow's ear. Being a success takes hard graft and that is our next ingredient.

Sir John Harvey-Jones was one of the first high-profile company chairmen to push the work-life balance agenda. Yet even he acknowledged:

> I am bound to admit that in terms of producing the balance of life which I would personally see as being the ideal, I have been relatively unsuccessful so far.[1]

The prime reason, he believed, that it is so difficult to find a balance between work and the rest of your life is that people at the top are expected to show their total personal commitment to a very large number of people – shareholders, employees, suppliers and customers.

This pressure is not confined to the business world. Many authors feel this pressure too. Having produced one or two popular books, an author now has to satisfy their agent, their publisher and their growing fan base with their next book. They cannot be complacent, but must get back to their desk and start writing again. When they stop, they feel guilty because people are looking to them for a result. Popular musicians often feel the same: they want to rest but instead commit to a gruelling world tour followed by six months in the studio producing their next album. There isn't an industry where success does not lead to more pressure to succeed . . . and to show you are working hard. We don't want to see our top people living it up on good food and good wine. We want to see them proving their worth.

In his book *Making It Happen*, Harvey Jones's description of the lifestyle of the most successful businesspeople – including 'sheer grinding brain power and the ability to live an intrinsically unhealthy existence', along with stressful travel that 'throws one's biological mechanisms into continual turmoil' – hardly sounds attractive.

Of course, as we have seen, people who are highly motivated to achieve success adapt their mindset so they do not see such a lifestyle as a sacrifice. They have chosen it and therefore they can live with the implications of that choice. Which isn't to say that they love waiting around in airports, getting home at midnight and attending working breakfasts at 6.30 a.m. It is hard work and seems, some-times, relentless.

I have clients who live in one city with their families but work in two other cities: they spend Monday to Wednesday in the North West head office and Thursday and Friday in the South East head office, only to return to the South West late on Friday night, exhausted, with a briefcase of work to complete by Monday and a packed schedule of children's activities to attend in the meantime. I have clients who regularly miss family holidays to attend international board meetings, returning to be with their loved ones for a few days in the middle of the vacation before jetting off to some other important engagement. I have clients who leave family and friends to take postings in far-flung parts of the world in order to further their career, and clients who work two or three jobs in order to fund their real passion for writing or art in the hope that, some day, their commitment will be recognised.

Sometimes trying to keep everything together in this mix proves impossible and family life cannot survive. Enabler Deborah Meredith, who has worked with many CEOs and company chairmen, says relationships only survive this pressure if the other partner is completely supportive:

> It is possible to have a rounded life if you have a supportive partner. Most of the men I have worked for had a wife who didn't work, or worked part-time. Dinner was on the table in the evening. At the weekend they would go out as a family and the children had all sorts of hobbies – horse-riding, sailing – so maybe there was an element of making up for some of the time that Dad wasn't around. But on the whole they were quite happy and had solid marriages. Only the owner-manager I worked for was divorced as a result of the business. Perhaps it is easier to keep your marriage together if you are an employee, a director or a partner, rather than the owner-manager.

Phil Taylor's job for Mattel involves considerable international travel and postings around the world. He says it is up to the individual to decide whether it is a price worth paying:

In my own situation I haven't paid a high price. I have a beautiful wife who sees my career path as an opportunity for herself
and the children. There is a spirit of adventure to it. We didn't
sit around at night thinking, 'I wish we could be in Indonesia',
and when the opportunity came up to live and work there we
had a two year old and my wife was pregnant with our second
child, but she said: 'This will come along once in your lifetime,
let's do it!' There's courage and spirit in that.

Research shows that many of us are working significantly longer
hours than in the past. One study of college-educated men working
full-time in the US found that those putting in a 50-hour week rose
from 22.2 per cent to 30.5 per cent between 1980 and 2001.[2] Sixty-
two per cent of high-earning individuals work more than 50 hours a
week, 35 per cent working more than 60 hours and 10 per cent
working more than 80 hours a week. A 60-hour week translates into
leaving the house at 7 a.m., commuting for an hour and then leaving
work at 8 p.m., arriving home at 9 p.m. This is probably quite typical
behaviour in the workplaces you have experienced.

In addition to showing your personal commitment to those you
work with there are other reasons why people's taste for working long
hours has increased since Sir John Harvey-Jones wrote his book
Making It Happen in 1988.

In 2005 there were 368 fewer corporate officer positions in
Fortune 500 companies than there had been 10 years before, which
means competition is that much greater. Add to this the influx of
women into the workforce over the past 50 years, and there are even
more people competing for fewer top jobs. At the same time, the
rewards at the very top are much greater than ever before. Multi-
million pound salaries and bonuses paid to CEOs and other board
members in some international companies mean there is the promise
of a big financial pay-off if you make it to the top. The same applies
in other fields: we've all heard of the Internet start-ups which make

millions for their 20-something founders when they are sold to Google or eBay. And we've all heard of the musicians, artists and writers who end up on *The Sunday* Times Rich List after a particularly good year. Working hard can pay off big time, if you can stand the heat.

Sylvia Ann Hewlett and Carolyn Buck Luce have coined a term for these kinds of high pressure, long-hours jobs – Extreme Jobs.[3] If you work more than 60 hours a week, are a high earner and hold a position with at least five of these characteristics you are in an Extreme Job:

- unpredictable flow of work;
- fast-paced work under tight deadlines;
- inordinate scope of responsibility that amounts to more than one job;
- work-related events outside regular work hours;
- availability to clients 24/7;
- responsibility for profit and loss;
- responsibility for mentoring and recruiting;
- large amount of travel;
- large number of direct reports;
- physical presence at workplace at least 10 hours a day.

They found that 21 per cent of high earners meet these Extreme Job criteria. In those who work in global companies the figure is 45 per cent. And the cost? Most Extreme Jobholders say that their job interferes with their ability to maintain a home, their relationship with their children, their relationship with their partner and even their sex life.

It isn't all bad news, though. Sixty-six per cent of people who hold an Extreme Job say that they love it. In global companies, the number is 76 per cent. These are people on a mission. They are passionate about what they do and see their long hours as a badge of honour. The vast majority say their hours are self-inflicted – they do it because they want to.

WHAT'S LUCK GOT TO DO WITH IT?

Successful people work hard because they want to. For most of them, it doesn't even feel like work most of the time. Given the choice between doing their job and practically anything else, they choose their work. As we have already seen, motivation is in large part connected with enjoyment of the work itself.

For these people the phrase 'work-life balance' has little meaning. Work is life, a big part of it anyway. They don't work to live but live to work. And this might be why so many successful people believe they have simply been lucky. They worked hard, but they enjoyed it so they barely noticed. And then, out of nowhere, came a great opportunity. And it is a phenomenon that Enabler Deborah Meredith has seen in her work many times:

> I think a lot of luck is down to hard work. But it might not feel like it because really successful people often forget they worked really hard. Sometimes you speak to the right person at an event by luck. But, of course, you have to be at the event in the first place and you have to go up to people and start conversations. People don't realise how much work they've put in to get into these situations.

Because they are focused on pursuing a dream, they are sometimes surprised that the pieces come together so neatly. It seems as if they were just in the right place at the right time.

Star Maker Carole Blake says that luck plays only a small part in most people's success recipe:

> Mostly people make their own luck. Sometimes people can disingenuously say, 'I was in the right place at the right time,' but for the most part we tailor the situations we find ourselves in. There is some wonderful luck sometimes. Very shortly after a famous seafaring author died, I took on Julian

Stockwin who was writing a seafaring series. The market was keen because the other writer had died. But, to be honest, I would have taken on this author anyway because I love his work.

The luck argument is actually most frequently heard from onlookers who want a no self-blame justification for their own lack of success. If a colleague was simply in the right place at the right time, then the result was out of their control. 'If I had been at that meeting, I would have come up with that idea and I would have got that promotion' say the wannabes. 'If I had got a big redundancy payment, I would have started my own business and made millions of pounds' or 'If my dad worked for the BBC, I would have got my own show and become famous.' What a perfect excuse for a lacklustre career!

In truth, events that look like lucky breaks occur frequently. What successful people (or people on their way to success) are able to do is to notice and take those opportunities. Key Holder Phil Taylor says he got a few lucky breaks. Of course, he put himself in the right place at the right time:

> Yes, there is a role for luck in success. But the real art is being brave enough to take the breaks when they are offered. It is about taking the opportunity. If I look at my own career, I've been lucky because the right things have come along. But, one, when the right things came along I had already done something to put myself in the position where other people think, 'Would you be interested in doing whatever?' I didn't decide they were going to build a second factory in Indonesia, but I had done something where they said, 'Hey, would you be interested in working on this project with us?' Two, I took advantage of it. That's not lucky. You have to have the initiative, the will, the gumption to take advantage of it. You make your own luck.

Unpredictable events, both good and bad, do occur of course. A vacancy opens at the perfect time for you, the economy shifts, a war breaks out somewhere, someone new comes to your company who takes a shine to you . . . I once got a great radio job because an editor thought I had potential. By the time I started the job, he had left and was replaced by someone who didn't see the same qualities in me! Too late. I was already there. Had the job been advertised a few weeks later when the new editor was in charge, I probably would have received a rejection letter (I eventually proved my worth, but it took time).

Star Maker Lucy Harris is looking for top-quality candidates to take lead roles in the retail industry. Luck is low down on her list of success ingredients:

> I believe you make your own luck. Unlucky things do happen and they are out of our control, but it's about how you bat those things away and get to the same end point. I think you can have a lucky break, but you might not have a lucky future. You are the master of your destiny.

Putting your success down to luck can leave a sour after-taste too. Quite common, even amongst seemingly self-confident, successful individuals is the 'fraud syndrome'. Some successful people are so unaware of their own qualities and achievements that they wonder why they are in a position of authority at all.

The 'fraud syndrome' concept is something which resonates with Enabler and strategist John Savage:

> There is quite a feeling of being fraudulent. Because it isn't enough to know what the answer is, you have to have the talent to make things happen. That requires courage. And when you start talking to a lot of people about a concept, when you are a leader, you can be sure there are 50 people

who don't agree with you. That exposes you. You don't want to get it wrong. That's where the anxiety comes from. But you have to remind yourself that this feeling is false. Courage isn't something you are born with, it is something you learn. You learn that you do something and it turns out alright and that it is worth making the effort, exposing yourself, taking the risk.

'Fraud syndrome' may assist some successful people in staying grounded. They believe, rightly or wrongly, that it makes them sensitive to others. They are aware of their own flaws and insecurities, so they accept that other people have flaws and insecurities. It may be an aspect of self-awareness which gives them a greater emotional intelligence.

Interestingly, 'fraud syndrome' – or the 'impostor phenomenon' as it was described by Georgia State University psychologists Pauline Clance and Suzanne Imes – is often found in individuals who come from families where parents are over-invested in achievement and where human warmth is lacking. In time, these people tend to turn into insecure overachievers.

It is also quite common in individuals who are not expected to succeed. In socially disadvantaged groups, parents may withhold encouragements because their children's ambitions seem unrealistic. Children who advance despite their background often have a lingering feeling about being 'above themselves' and wonder how long their success will last.[4] It seems as though the very aspect of their background which contributed so much to their desire to succeed also prevents them from enjoying it very much.

WORKING ON THE INSIDE

This may be why so many successful people are interested in self-development. They know that lacking confidence, doubting your self-worth and constantly fearing being found out can limit your enjoyment of success and, eventually, wear you down so much that it starts to impact your performance.

When successful people feel that they are holding themselves back, they seek feedback. Because they are people of action, they don't spend weeks and months stuck in a rut. They notice a pattern and take action, very often by consulting people they respect or referring to written material for answers. Successful people aren't just working hard at the day job. They are working hard on themselves too.

They want to know more about themselves. This isn't because they are self-obsessed (or rather, it isn't always because they are self-obsessed), but because they know that self-awareness is the key to better performance. Many read publications like the *Harvard Business Review* to get the latest thinking on being a better leader, on improving their management skills, or on working more effectively with others. They need to know what makes themselves tick in order to understand what makes others tick and how to get the best from the people around them.

They might not go on meditation retreats or learn Qi-Gong or other soothing martial arts (although some do), but they still pursue their own interests in personal development. However, they often don't advertise the fact. This work is often private and only communicated when there is a political advantage to be had from admitting frailty or flaws.

Becoming successful is not about accidentally landing in the right place at exactly the right moment, getting discovered on the street or walking in to *The X Factor* auditions without having shown any interest in singing before. It is about putting in the hours, burning the midnight oil, being proactive and the many other clichés which are so common because they are true. If you aren't willing to put in the work, you are either in the wrong career or simply not motivated enough to achieve success at the highest level.

There is nothing wrong with that. Not everyone can be Chief

Executive, Number One Bestseller or Prime Minister. Not everyone wants to. But if you do, there are a few extra ingredients you will need to add flavour to your dish.

GRAFT RECIPE

- Work-life balance is not an integral part of the success recipe; successful people don't think in these terms. Work is a major part of life, not something relegated to the nine to five.
- If you can't stand the heat, get out of the kitchen. If you aren't prepared to regularly choose work over other aspects of life, you won't get ahead.
- Relationships can be part of the success mix if your other half is supportive and flexible.
- Successful people don't wait for luck to strike. They make their own.
- 'Fraud syndrome' can slip in to the success recipe if you haven't dealt with issues from the past.
- Success is a holistic pursuit. You need to work on your inner game as well as your day job.

REFERENCES

1 Harvey-Jones, John. *Making It Happen: Reflections on Leadership*. p.285. London: Fontana/Collins, 1988.

2 Hewlett, Sylvia, and Carolyn Buck Luce. 'The Dangerous Allure of the 70-Hour Workweek'. p.51. *Harvard Business Review*, December 2006. [Research by Peter Kuhn and Fernando Lozano of the National Bureau of Economic Research.]

3 Hewlett, Sylvia, and Carolyn Buck Luce. 'The Dangerous Allure of the 70-Hour Workweek'. p.51. *Harvard Business Review*, December 2006.

4 Kets de Vries, Manfred F. R. 'The Dangers of Feeling Like a Fake'. p.110. *Harvard Business Review*, September 2005.

Ingredient 11

Seasoning

Everyone has their own personal taste when it comes to the recipe for success. Some of our experts stressed 'steel' over and above every other ingredient; others thought manners were most vital. Still others wanted to emphasise the ability to build trust.

And in addition to the ten ingredients described already, some of our experts wanted to pepper the recipe with their own special blend of herbs and spices. These ingredients aren't necessarily secondary. After all, a curry without the seasoning is just a plate of meat and veg. You may find that the key to your success lies in the ingredients in this chapter either because you feel you are already working on all the others or because something in this chapter just tickles your taste buds. These are added extras that at least one of the experts mentioned as being important.

VISION

Vision is mentioned in every leadership handbook and at every company away-day, so it would be remiss of me to leave it out of this book. The ability to imagine the big picture future and engage people in support of it is vital in any profession and any industry. Think it doesn't matter in the music business? Of course it does. The most successful stars aren't one-hit wonders, because they have engaged their audience in something bigger. They are 'saying something', they have a message or they make people feel a certain way (excited, positive, understood or rebellious for instance).

In fact, because musicians do this without standing at a podium in front of PowerPoint slides but through the emotional medium of song, we actually feel even more drawn to their vision than we do in a more conventional presentation. Where most aspiring leaders (and many who are already in the top spot) go wrong is that they do not connect with us on an emotional level. It's all mission statements and value propositions.

Having 'vision' in the corporate world tends to translate into creating a one-sentence statement which sums up the purpose of the business or project or piece of work. Here are some examples I found on the Internet.

- **To provide high-quality products that combine performance with value pricing, while establishing a successful relationship with our customers and our suppliers;**
- **To constantly strive to meet or exceed our customer needs and expectations of price, service, and selection. To this end, we will perform periodic reviews of the marketplace to improve our offerings;**
- **To stay ahead of the competition by innovating new products and services based on the needs of our customers and market demand.**

Do you want to work for these companies? Do these statements get you really fired up? Do you even know what they mean? Most people in large organisations don't know that these statements exist. If they do, they don't feel any connection with them and they don't understand where they fit in relation to them.

Most people cannot connect with these statements because their job function isn't included in the statement. How can the reception staff or the IT help desk or the people in accounts 'perform periodic reviews of the marketplace'? It doesn't have anything to do with them on a daily basis. And even those in the business who have direct contact with customers will spend a great deal of their time doing activities that don't relate to 'innovating new products and services'. How do you expect them to remain motivated and focused when they are sitting in yet another meeting discussing changes to the office space or problems with the company intranet?

Not everyone is naturally visionary. Some people are great at working through a list of jobs. They are efficient, very effective and certainly hardworking, but they cannot picture or feel what the future should be like. Can you connect with something in your work that gets you excited and gives you butterflies in your stomach when you think of it? If you can't, you certainly won't be able to inspire others.

A great vision often comes in two parts.

Core Ideology

What lies at the core of your work? What are the values that guide every single aspect of your behaviour and the behaviour of the people around you? This is the part of your vision which provides inspiration and probably aspiration (you may not be there yet but you are aiming for it). It is your *core ideology* – what you or your business stands for. It should never have to change. Some of the most successful businesses in the word have adapted immensely to changing technology and products without losing their core ideology. Hewlett-Packard has the HP Way which, despite changes in operating practices, culture and business strategy, remains constant. The HP Way, which was seen as radical when it was first developed, was the belief that employees' brainpower was the company's most important resource. Many companies claim they put employees first but at HP the right of employees to work in an environment where they can contribute their brainpower is a powerful and inspirational core ideology.

The diversified technology company 3M still commits to solving unsolved problems innovatively even though it has changed direction and sold off many successful parts of the company over the years.[1]

Both of these are examples of core ideologies which can inspire staff, shareholders and customers.

Envisioned Future

The second part of a vision is the *envisioned future* – a 10 to 30-year Big Fat Audacious Goal with a description of how it will feel to get there. It must be compelling and measurable. People need to know when they have arrived at their destination. Henry Ford described a world where everyone with a good salary could afford a car and horses would disappear from the streets. Audacious, risky, visionary but, in the end, a reality. A vision should make us tingle and get to us in an emotional way rather than relating to profit and loss.

How a vision is expressed makes all the difference. The cleaning staff at an American theme park I know of felt hugely stressed and unhappy whenever visitors dropped litter on the ground. They would make a face and reluctantly clear the mess, often making the visitors feel uncomfortable because of their attitude. They had been told that their job was to 'keep the place tidy', so every time someone undid their hard work they were, naturally, displeased. The boss spent some time with the cleaning staff and noticed their building frustration. He decided to change the message to 'create a fantastic experience for our visitors'. By keeping the site clean they were contributing to that vision. Picking up litter was one of the ways they could improve the visitor experience, as was being helpful with directions, smiling at people and taking pride in their work.

Successful people are honest when they create and communicate their vision. I have been to many companies which claim to 'put our people first'. In truth, they put profit first, perhaps shareholder needs second, keeping customers happy third and trying to keep their staff happy last. There is nothing wrong with this order of priority. What is wrong is that the leaders of the company are misleading when they insist that they value their staff as their greatest asset. When the professed 'brand values' of the company are in contrast to the reality of working there, people become disillusioned. Far better to be frank. If shareholder value is number one, look at why – what lies at the root of that priority? – and create a vision which inspires your people to want to work towards that end.

Successful people not only have a vision, but are able to engage people behind a vision. They may not be great orators who rally all the staff at the annual Christmas party. They may work in more subtle ways, meeting with small groups or even holding one-to-ones. And they walk the talk. They behave in ways that are congruent with their message. If the vision relates to how staff should be treated in the workplace, successful leaders do not bend or break the rules. They stick with them even if that puts them in an uncomfortable position sometimes.

Of course, on your way up the ladder you may not be able to influence the vision. You may just be tasked with communicating it. Worst case scenario, you don't even know what it is. Well, get to know what it is and find a way to express it that can inspire people around you. If you can't get behind it because it goes against what you believe, you may need to find another job. You will not be successful in an environment which conflicts with your values. However, the current company vision is probably so meaningless that you can interpret it however you like and start getting people engaged behind that interpretation.

And if you aren't in big business, start to consciously envision your core ideology and future. Write it down or illustrate it in pictures. Try to clarify it without losing its essence. Successful artists can usually describe their vision, or it is implicit in their work. It's the same with people who start their own companies and go on to have great success. They have clarity around their vision and are able to communicate it to others. Not through a mission statement full of bland words and even blander sentiment, but by pulling at our heart strings or finding something which resonates with our values.

LOSE THE EGO

Top chef Gordon Ramsay changed jobs a lot in his early professional career in the kitchen. He wanted to work in a variety of leading restaurants and learn skills from a variety of great cooks. Every time he went to a new kitchen, armed with his previous experience, he started at the bottom again, chopping vegetables.

This attitude, from a chef known for his strong personality, shows that he was not motivated by his ego. He knew that he had to prove himself to each new boss. His achievements in his previous kitchen were of interest, but his new leader wanted him to start from scratch, learning their way rather than bringing habits from another kitchen to his work. He eagerly accepted this reality, knowing he would end up armed with a range of approaches and be able to choose which one he wanted to promote in his own kitchen. Now, with numerous Michelin stars to his name, it seems to have paid off.

It is a quality that Mattel's Phil Taylor rates very highly:

I took a risk going to Hong Kong when many people didn't really understand why the job should be there. And then I proved myself successful at that level so they asked if I wanted to come to Europe. Some people would say, 'Why do I have to prove myself again?' You've got to be prepared to say new boss, new environment, new job. You've got to prove your credibility again. You have to think, 'If that's what I need to do to carry on this path, then that's what I need to do. OK, fine. I will prove it again. No problem.' It's not a risk because you know you can do it. It is self-confidence.

The only reason people fight this requirement to prove themselves time and time again is insecurity. If they are truly confident that they can demonstrate their skill, they will happily show anyone who asks what they can do.

Sometimes they are being asked to prove their ability out of a genuine need. People often make over-inflated statements about themselves ('I have what it takes to be the next winner of *The X Factor*'), but until we see what they can do we cannot be sure. Words are not enough. Just watch contestants on *The Apprentice* claiming to 'lead from the front' or be a 'people person' and then behave in completely contradictory ways. Key Holders, Enablers and Star Makers need proof, not empty claims.

Sometimes they are being asked to prove their ability as a test of attitude. Those who resist are showing that they are not willing to play the game, something which looks like bad manners. Individuals who resist playing this game may think they are simply standing up for themselves and believe that this quality will be admired. But what most employers are looking for is people who will muck in.

At times of recession this is particularly important. Research into the behaviours which are most likely to keep you employed when redundancies are being made shows that people who are ambidextrous and willing to do two jobs at once when times are tough will be more secure than those who resist.[2] In time, those people will be able to influence change in the business. But, for now, they are being asked to show their commitment to the team. If this means pitching in and doing jobs that are 'beneath' them, they need to simply roll up their sleeves and get on with it.

DEALING WITH FAILURE

We have already seen that successful people all have failures in their past. They may have failed business or returned manuscripts, rejection letters or marriages that didn't stand the pressure, but they do not see themselves as failures. And, in most cases, they do not consider these events as failure. They regard failure as a learning opportunity. Without falling over, a baby would never learn to walk. Failure forces us to try different methods and, through trial and error, we find what works for us. It is only if we give up that failure marks the end, rather than a waypoint along the route to success. In fact, in truly innovative environments, failure is encouraged. At Google the mantra is 'Please fail very quickly – so that you can try again'.[3]

Jerry Hirshberg was the founder of Nissan Design International, a design lab set up by Nissan in the US to originate fresh, revolutionary ideas for motor vehicles. After some years, success meant the lab doubled in size and new designers joined the team. Problems which had never been there before started to emerge. Tensions and conflicts led to product ideas which received cool responses from the Japanese headquarters.

Hirshberg believes that the old team had become set in its ways after a very short period of time and the new team members had noticed. By identifying what was going wrong he and his people were able to correct it:

> Confronting our errors openly, overcoming our defensiveness and embarrassment and modelling the same behaviours we were expecting from the staff all helped to reinforce an atmosphere tolerant of failure. It also enabled us to open doors that would have remained closed, at least until the greater and more costly failures that might have occurred had we continued on our original path. This can only happen in a culture more concerned with the potential lurking in failure than in the mere avoidance of its repercussions.[4]

Most organisations, in fact most people, try to avoid failure as much as possible. They focus on what they know will work and try to patch up problems. They are afraid to open a can of worms if they delve too deeply, preferring to believe they will go away of their own accord or never bubble up to the surface and cause overt issues.

That is normally fine when things are going well, but when times are tough, problems often blow up, in the shape of average products that do not fully satisfy customers, workplace dynamics that mean teams are not fully effective and oversights that mean accounting procedures are less than accurate.

Headhunter and Star Maker Lucy Harris says that the ability to look failure in the eye is a particularly important quality today:

> As a general rule, top people are having to deal with more failure this year than ever before. They are encouraged that they are not alone. If they are in charge of a sinking ship, they know they have done everything within their power and their remit to save it and this helps make that failure more understandable. Some characters deal with it better than others. Some are able to understand where they went wrong and others can't see where they were accountable at all. Failure is something you learn from. Having said that, it does mean there are casualties, so hopefully you are learning so that it doesn't have to happen again.

Not only do successful people accept, analyse and even embrace failure, but they do the same with success. When things turn out as well as expected or better than expected, we tend to celebrate without really understanding why things went right. Asking, 'Where did it all go right?' can help you to learn from success, so it can be repeated, and even to see where success could have been greater. As athlete Sebastian Coe once remarked, 'If you don't know why you've failed, how can you improve? And if you don't know why you succeeded, it must have been an accident.'[5]

THEY DO WHAT IT TAKES

In 2007, more than 32,000 cosmetic procedures were carried out in the UK, an increase of 12 per cent on the previous year. Surgery on men increased by 17.5 per cent with many of them having nose jobs. Breast augmentation was the most popular surgery for women.[6]

These figures come as no surprise to image consultant Sharon

Connolly. How you look matters. People believe that looking younger and more attractive will help their prospects which, in turn, will help them feel better about themselves. If you want to get ahead, and you are fat, lose weight, she says:

> People who are hugely driven will also change their physical appearance by working out or having surgery to fit this ideal. If you are overweight, lose some weight. Fat people are assumed to be lazy. Beautiful people are already a few steps up the ladder.

While it is not vital to be a slim size 12 or to look like George Clooney, increasingly men and women are going under the knife in order to conform to an image they believe will be more acceptable. Top dogs used to invest in a high-quality toupee in order to appear more 'with it'. This may just be the next step.

Of course, most successful people have not had surgery and certainly wouldn't recommend it as the way to progress. However, what these numbers show is that some people are willing to compete in any way they can. They will not exclude a tactic if they think it will work and if it fits with their values. They are willing to do what it takes. And it is this general attitude which separates those who get to the top from those who do not.

Many people choose, consciously or unconsciously, not to go any further because they are not willing to do what it takes. For them, especially where the choice was a conscious one, stopping at middle management, or with a healthy business making a nice profit or with a top 100 bestselling book is enough. Going further would mean sacrificing values they believe are important and this matters more to them than achieving conventional measures of success. If you are not willing to do what it takes, then you are making a decision to go no further. This is perfectly healthy, but may explain why your more ambitious colleagues are rising up the ranks more quickly than you.

ENJOYMENT

Most of the experts interviewed for this book agreed that successful people are having fun. Despite (or perhaps because of) the pressure, the long hours, the responsibility and the risks, they do it because they want to. Phil Taylor says:

> The ability to make a difference, the ability to shape and form a direction . . . If you don't enjoy this kind of thing, you are in the wrong job.

And this enjoyment may be why they are so unstoppable, according to Enabler Vicki Day:

> It isn't about 'the greater glory' or going down in history. I can't imagine Einstein thinking, 'This will make me a million.' They just have an idea and want to see it to fruition. They want to prove they were right, and that's more important than being rich or famous. Today's children just want to be famous for being famous. They don't have a USP. Whereas someone like Richard Branson . . . if Virgin crashed he would go off to his island for one last holiday and probably come up with another idea, go back to the UK and do that.

Deborah Meredith agrees, believing that what successful people enjoy is the never-ending nature of their quest:

> I haven't met anyone who has achieved what they wanted to achieve and been unhappy. But even then they are still striving for more. Some people will determine their success by material things and those people may not be happy. But people who are constantly looking to better themselves, improve themselves may never be quite satisfied but they are probably happy.

Knowing what makes you happy is key to deciding how successful to become. The never ending quest doesn't work for everyone. For some, the prospect of one day retiring and taking it easy is highly motivating and the perpetual battle to stay ahead of the rest would become wearisome, even boring and perhaps put great strain on their health. And, of course, once you understand what makes you happy, you can devise your own definition of success. In this book we have assumed success needs to include great wealth, high status or renown. But you can define success by different criteria – those based on what gives meaning and satisfaction to your life.

SEASONING TIPS

- Some success dishes are all about the seasoning. If your recipe is lacking flavour, it might need a good dash of something spicy.
- Seasoning should suit your own taste, but also the needs of your business or industry. At certain times, some of these ingredients are more in demand than at others. And tastes are constantly changing.
- Remember not to overdo the seasoning. Vision is all very well but there must be substance behind it. By all means have cosmetic surgery if you want to, but keep it subtle. Too much can be worse than doing nothing at all.

REFERENCES

1 Collins, James C., and Jerry I. Porras. 'Building Your Company's Vision'. p.1. *Harvard Business Review*, Sep/Oct 1996.
2 Banks, Janet, and Diane Coutu. 'How to Protect Your Job in a Recession'. p.114. *Harvard Business Review*, September 2008.
3 Davenport, Thomas H., and Bala Iyer. 'Reverse Engineering Google's Innovation Machine'. p.66. *Harvard Business Review*, April 2008.
4 Hirshberg, Jerry. *The Creative Priority*. p.116. London: HarperBusiness, 1998.
5 In private conversation with author, Jeff Grout.
6 www.news-medical.net/?id=34880 [Research by The British Association of Aesthetic Plastic Surgeons (**www.baaps.org.uk**), the not-for-profit organisation established for the advancement of education and practice of Aesthetic Plastic Surgery for public benefit.]

Ingredient 12

Poisons

We could call this chapter 'What *Not* to Do If You Want to Be Successful', but it doesn't roll off the tongue as easily as 'Poisons'. You can have heaped tablespoons of the ingredients in this book and then add one of these poisons and ruin the whole dish. Just as there are behaviours and qualities that Star Makers, Key Holders and Enablers want to see in their prodigies, there are also behaviours and qualities they really do not want to see.

The most obvious of these are the unpleasant or even unacceptable characteristics often highlighted in media portrayals of successful people. And, believe it or not, some wannabes take their cue from the 'You're fired' approach they see on everything from *The Apprentice* to *The X Factor*. 'Take out the opposition, using whatever means possible' has become the Holy Grail of what it takes to be successful and, as a coach, I have certainly witnessed individuals who emulate this style in the mistaken belief that they will be admired, respected and promoted on the basis of their hard-nosed attitude.

It is certainly true that the 10 key ingredients we have seen so far have more than a little 'edginess' about them. Having good manners is not the same as being a pushover. Successful people are tough-minded and determined and they do not let individuals, organisations or societal pressure get in their way if they believe in what they are doing, but that doesn't mean they are nasty. They may act in ways which would go against your own personal code of conduct.

However, according to our experts at least, most successful people are moral, genuine and honest (within the rules of play that exist in their industry). They tend to treat people well (those who matter to them, at least) and typically pursue success for more than just personal gain – they may want to succeed for their family, their employees, their supporters or the greater good.

It can be a hard life with tough choices along the way and many make what we would consider to be sacrifices in order to achieve their goals. This means there may be some 'wounded souls' along the way, victims of the successful person's determined pursuit of achievement. However, few successful people get pleasure from this aspect, most try to avoid injury being caused to other people and, while they may accept it as inevitable, many go out of their way to minimise the cost to others of their ambition. They certainly do not set out to harm anyone and this is certainly not where they get their pleasure.

Poisons come in two forms. They are those behaviours which are intended to cause pain or unhappiness in others – bullying, lying or personal vendettas for instance. And then there are those more subtle poisons based on oversights, selfishness or insecurity which cause avoidable damage to others and which will also get in the way of getting ahead.

It is this second form of poison we are going to focus on, on the assumption that you already know if you are being intentionally mean and nothing I say here is going to stop you.

LACK OF GENEROSITY

One ingredient which can limit a person's success is lack of generosity. Key Holder Oli Barrett goes out of his way sometimes to help people but finds, occasionally, that others are not willing to acknowledge him in return:

> There is a lack of generosity sometimes with people you have helped who don't help you back. They often do quite well, but

don't end up making a success of all areas of their life. They are not interested in people, so people are not interested in them.

In a way, these people are demonstrating the exact opposite of the good manners that so many of our experts rated as vital. Such lack of generosity doesn't guarantee failure, but it may mean it is more difficult to succeed. Without other people's help, life is a struggle and you have to fight for absolutely everything on your own.

Most successful people have spent many years networking. They know that success often comes down to who you know. Where there is a pre-existing trusting relationship, you are more likely to get the job, get the contract or get the deal. Those who network effectively don't have a single 'win' in mind. They don't head straight over to Joe Bloggs, the owner of a large manufacturing company, when they see him at a business lunch and thrust their card in his hand while delivering a monologue about their inventive new product. Instead, they build their network over time. They become well known and well respected in their industry or their circle. They are generous with their time and earn the trust of influential and powerful people, often by giving help and advice and asking for little in return. When the time comes that they need help in return, other people are more than willing to lend a hand, if the project is worthy.

Of course, such behaviour is rarely motivated by pure altruism. Great networkers know that their groundwork will pay dividends later on. They know that the bigger and more solid their network, the more opportunities are likely to come their way. All they have to do then is prove they have the ability to do what they say they can do.

However, some people network with purely selfish motives. They are after a quick win. They have no intention of giving anything up front which would prove their commitment. They expect you to give them something first and, surprise, surprise, when you ask for something back they are nowhere to be seen. This is looked upon very poorly and word tends to get around. In terms of David Maister's 'Four Dimensions of Trust',[1] this kind of behaviour scores badly all around. The individual loses credibility because people cannot trust what he says. He has not demonstrated any track record and has not taken any action to prove he will do what he says, so he is therefore perceived as unreliable. People begin to feel uncomfortable discussing things with him, so the intimacy is gone. And when they ask, 'What does this person care about?' the answer is always 'Himself'.

The world of work can be a tough, even ruthless place. But there are still rules of behaviour which are upheld by most, and give and take is one of those. Lack of generosity will certainly taint your recipe.

LIMITING BELIEFS

I have met many ambitious individuals who believe the world is against them. They are motivated by the desire to show everyone they are right and everyone else is wrong. They have many of the qualities mentioned so far, but their belief system is holding them back. When we believe that the world is out to get us, we look for evidence that this is true. Unconsciously, we may even create scenarios in order to prove ourselves right. Let's take the fictional example of Andrew.

Andrew believes that life is tough, people are selfish and everyone is against him. He goes to the bank to get a business loan. He is convinced that the bank will turn him down, so he is immediately on the defensive. When they ask him questions about the business, he believes they are trying to find flaws in his idea and gives short, aggressive answers. When the bank manager asks where else he has looked for financing, he lists a large number of people and institutions who turned him down, remarking that they were short-sighted idiots. Inevitably, the bank decides he is not a good risk and declines him a loan, thus proving to Andrew that they had no intention of helping him and were just wasting his time for the fun of it.

An over-exaggeration of course. But our attitudes do influence our behaviours, so it is worth knowing what yours are. If you believe that people won't help you, you will give up after the third person has said no. If you believe people will help you, you keep looking until someone says yes. If you believe in 'paying it forward' (I do something good for someone and perhaps something good happens to me), then you notice when good things happen and this reinforces your belief.

Common limiting beliefs include:

- **I am not good enough;**
- **good things don't happen to me;**
- **I am unlucky;**
- **everybody hates me;**
- **people are just after a quick buck;**
- **people cannot be trusted;**
- **life is hard;**
- **bad things happen to good people;**
- **it will never work.**

Do any of these feel familiar? It is worth assessing what your beliefs are about yourself and about the world. If you aren't sure, ask other people. They may be able to see your limiting assumptions more clearly than you.

It is possible to create new assumptions or beliefs which will help you progress. Let's say you perceive yourself as unlucky. Because we tend to justify our limiting beliefs by drawing on the evidence that they are true, you will have a very clear memory of all the times you have been unlucky. And that reinforces your belief that you are not a lucky person. You can then blame this for your lack of success. However, if you change your beliefs and decide that you *are* lucky, you will start looking for evidence that this is true. Every time something lucky happens, make a note of it. Look for the luck in everything. Before long you will start to feel like a lucky person and have no more excuses for holding yourself back (I am not a great believer in luck as a success ingredient, as you will have seen. So instead of seeing yourself as unlucky, you could see yourself as someone who doesn't believe in luck. This might be a more powerful and useful shift.)

MOTIVATION MISPLACEMENT

People who succeed are generally doing something they believe in. They put themselves at the centre of their motivation. This is not to say that they are selfish in the negative sense. They do not disregard other people. As we have seen earlier in this chapter, people who care only about themselves do not generate trust by others, and most successful people care about more than themselves and their own gratification. But they are getting their own needs met through pursuing a particular professional path. Star Maker and headhunter Lucy Harris says:

> They know their goals and they go for them. Part of that is selfish. They are self-aware about their needs and how to supply those needs.

When this is missing because they put everyone else's needs ahead of their own, their motivation may still be high, but it may also be unhealthy, causing them significant damage and taking a serious negative toll over time.

Adrian Moorhouse and Professor Graham Jones have seen misplaced motivations in both sportspeople and businesspeople. In the context of discussing young sportspeople whose parents have invested heavily in them (in all senses), as Professor Jones puts it:

> These performers are very aware of their parents' desires for their success and have been 'doing it for them' rather than to

satisfy their own needs. This does not bode well for long-term participation or even enjoyment.[2]

Putting other people's needs before your own can manifest itself in a number of ways. People who do this often worry about appearing selfish and so they go to the other extreme. They may not like to disagree with people and worry about hurting people's feelings. They stay in situations which do not work well for them and play down their accomplishments. They sacrifice themselves for the sake of other people and under-value their own worth. Such behaviour sometimes begins as an act (deep down you know you are fabulous, but you also know that telling people may make you unpopular), then over time you begin to believe it. Just as 'acting as if' you are confident can bring you the results of a confident person and in turn make you feel genuinely more confident, 'acting as if' you are not worthy can bring you the results of someone who is not worthy and make you feel genuinely worthless.

But whether this habit of putting others' needs first started with a lack of self-confidence or developed because you acted as if you didn't matter and eventually became unconfident, disregarding your own needs is certain to ruin your recipe for success. You put huge pressure on yourself by taking responsibility for the well-being of others over and above your own well-being. Not only do you have to contend with the ups and downs of your journey in terms of your own emotions, but you have to handle the emotions of other people who are looking to you for their happiness.

In reality, no matter how much you try you cannot guarantee other people's happiness. But by getting your own needs met and achieving your personal and professional goals you become an inspirational, interesting and fun person to be around. You have resources which you can share with other people and you have energy which you can put into people or causes you care about. That is a far more reliable way of bringing happiness to others.

LOSING PERSPECTIVE

Most ambitious people start off with a clear moral code. They know what they want to do, they know the values that motivate them and they hold themselves to certain standards of behaviour which they believe will not only help them achieve their personal goal, but achieve a greater good.

However, it is common to lose sight of this as you progress. The culture of whatever industry you work within is powerful. The music industry, the literary industry, the business community, the artistic community . . . they all have their own values, codes of behaviour and centres of power. In order to achieve success, one sometimes has to be flexible, but there is a line between flexibility and abandonment of your own core values.

Losing your perspective happens subtly, over time. Maybe you get drawn in to the 'presenteeism' culture. You stay behind late at the office because everyone else does. You create work to do in that time so that you seem busy and important. Instead of fighting the culture you play along, reinforcing it. When the time comes for you to be the boss, you are so entrenched in this culture that you no longer question it. And so it is perpetuated. Perhaps you began your working life with the belief that it was possible to find a healthy balance between time in the office and time outside. By the time you are in charge, this is a distant memory.

Maybe you get drawn into 'bad politics'. It begins as a way to bring about the changes you believe in. You leak some information to powerful decision-makers, compromising someone's privacy, but justifying it as a way to challenge the stagnant status quo. Over time your personal standards become eroded. It is now the norm for you to play this game and it has become almost impossible to go back. In fact, you come to believe that you were simply naïve and now that you have more experience you understand the real way of the world.

While it may not be possible or even advisable to hold on to everything you believed when you first began, assuming you do learn along the way and revise some of your simplistic attitudes as you mature, a great obstacle to success is losing touch with yourself and your values.

It is still possible to reach the top. But on reaching the top many people complain that it isn't what they expected. It does not feel like they thought it would. They expected to be able to change things once they got there, but now they are so much a part of the system that they cannot change it without also calling their own behaviour into question.

And losing sight of your values is a false economy. Fairness saves businesses money. Let's say that two organisations need to make redundancies. The first handles it badly saying to those who are being let go that they don't want to do this, but they have to, and then not being available to answer questions or explain the reasons for the job losses because they are uncomfortable and want to avoid confrontation. Consequently, there are numerous claims of unfair dismissal and even workers who keep their jobs are unhappy and their performance suffers.

The second explains the strategic purpose of the layoffs and managers at all levels make themselves available to any employee who wants to talk, argue or complain about the decision. Very few workers make unfair dismissal claims and workers who remain understand why the decisions were made, even if they are unhappy about the outcome, and return to their high performance levels rapidly. One unfair dismissal case can cost £50,000 or more, so handling it fairly, honestly and bravely can certainly save a great deal of money.[3]

If they were being honest, I am sure the managers in the first company would admit that they ducked out and compromised their values because it was hard work to live by them.

John Savage believes staying true to your values is vital if you are to make good decisions:

So much of life is about dialogue. If you inhibit people's willingness to get into that dialogue, you reduce your ability to gather information. The first requirement to live a good life is to understand the difference between truth and falsehood. You can't do that if you have created barriers, or if people are in awe of you or jealous of you.

There are a number of questions you can ask yourself to ensure that you are keeping your perspective.[4]

1. **Am I being true to myself?** Ask yourself whether your actions reflect who you truly are, whether you have become more tentative, politically correct or cautious because you don't want to risk losing that promotion, bonus or contract.
2. **Am I communicating?** Do people around you know what you stand for and what is important to you? Maybe there is some reason why you are reluctant to tell others what is in your mind. Perhaps this is because you find it hard to justify to yourself, let alone to others.
3. **How am I spending my time?** Have you become drawn into firefighting or 'busy' activities because it is easier than dealing with what is really important to you? Successful people stay focused on what is important. Are you?
4. **Am I open to feedback?** It is easy to close your ears to what other people are saying about you and justify this by thinking, 'I am not here to be popular, I am here to get things done.' But staying open to feedback will keep you true to yourself, even if it is hard to hear.
5. **Am I helping others to grow?** Your success relies on other people. Fear can motivate you to pull up the ladder behind you in the hope that subordinates or colleagues will not overtake you. But truly confident people help other people to achieve their potential knowing that this is no threat to them or their position.

6. **Am I still open to ideas?** The world is constantly changing, but you may have become stuck in your ways. Look around you and listen to new perspectives so you do not become part of the old order.

7. **How do I behave under pressure?** Over time, stress builds. Events which may not have flustered you in the past may start to get under your skin and your reactions may be out of proportion. Ask yourself what types of events create pressure for you and how your reactions might be undermining your success.

Those who are able to keep their perspective, live by their values and hold on to their moral code are not only more fulfilled when they reach the top, but are able to bring about changes in culture which benefit everyone and maybe save or make their business a fair bit of money too.

POISONS RECIPE

- If you want to poison yourself and possibly others, take help when it is offered but never help anyone in return. This is a guaranteed way to destroy trust and discourage those who are able to give you a leg up.
- Ask yourself how your beliefs are holding you back. Do they help you achieve your goals or sabotage your efforts? Get rid of limiting assumptions and replace them with positive ones which will aid your progress.
- A sure way to sour any success you achieve is to do it purely for other people. Disregarding your own needs in order to try to satisfy other people will adversely affect your enjoyment of success and is unlikely ever to be quite to the taste of those you are trying to please.

> • Over time, a great recipe can become bland or even go off completely. Keep your core values and moral code alive by checking in with yourself regularly and taking an honest, critical look at what you're doing. Do not lose sight of what you wanted to achieve and why.

REFERENCES

1 http://davidmaister.com/podcasts.archives/5/55
2 Jones, Graham, and Adrian Moorhouse. *Developing Mental Toughness: Gold Medal Strategies for Transforming Your Business Performance.* p.116. Oxford: Spring Hill, 2007.
3 Brockner, Joel. 'Why It's So Hard to Be Fair'. p.124. *Harvard Business Review*, March 2006.
4 Kaplan, Robert S. 'What to Ask the Person in the Mirror'. pp.90–91. *Harvard Business Review*, January 2007.

Chapter 13

Combining the ingredients

As I've been writing this book, I've discovered that success isn't a single 'destination'. You don't get there and then sit back to enjoy the view. Those who dream of success might imagine it as achieving a lifelong ambition which is so fulfilling that it is 'enough'. They think that once they have it, they'll feel satiated, full. Indeed part of its attraction is the belief that they'll finally feel complete, that an itch has been scratched, and that they can relax.

But just like our appetite, the 'full' feeling doesn't last for long. Successful people are only as successful as this morning's share price or this week's bestseller list. Success is a fleeting moment, a waypoint along a journey. Successful people certainly notice what they have achieved, with the help of those around them, and they may even enjoy the fruits of their success for a little while. They may take a holiday, buy a Ferrari or give themselves a pay rise. But then they get back to work, creating a bigger goal, a harder journey, a more challenging ride which may, in time, be followed by another fleeting feeling of success . . . before the whole process kicks off again.

Ironically, the dream of reaching the end of the journey is not the primary motivator for successful people. What they enjoy is the process of aiming for, and striving towards, success. They may achieve their original goals but by then they have already moved the goalposts further away. As soon as they get close to a goal they change it, enlarge it and make it ambitious, so they are never finished.

Along the journey there are moments when it feels good and moments when it feels bad. On a difficult day – having to make staff redundant, say – a 'successful' person is unlikely to feel like that. 'Success' becomes terminology that only the outsider looking on would use.

As tycoon Peter Jones says:

> The truth is that everyone will experience successes and failures in their business life. All you can hope for is that you are able to tip the balance in favour of the former.[1]

When I asked some of our experts whether they perceived them-selves as successful, they all replied 'marginally' – despite being leaders in their field with a proven track record. They have had successes but because they do not perceive themselves as a finished product, they cannot judge whether they themselves are successful.

This is why it is vital to enjoy the journey. And you can choose what kind of journey that is, so that it remains a true reflection of your values, your code of conduct and your priorities. Keeping your head down and compromising on what you believe in for 10 or 20 years in the belief that when you get the big prize it will all have been worth it is a huge price to pay if, once you become CEO or Number One in the charts, it doesn't feel like enough.

Armed with the ingredients for success you now have to blend them together to create your own unique recipe. Getting the balance right will be, in part, a case of trial and error. You may focus initially on honing your talent and letting the other ingredients simmer quietly in the background only to find, in a couple of years, that the next stage in your career requires more networking – building trust, developing your own kitchen cabinet and playing the politics game. You may believe you need to focus on putting in the hours, thinking this is what will give your recipe the extra spice it needs, only to discover that in your industry – or due to your personality – graft is less significant than good manners.

It is fine to keep adapting and adjusting your recipe until you find the right combination for you. But you can apply some structure to the decisions you make about what to focus on and what to emphasise right now as you embark on your journey.

This is where the INW theory may be useful. INW stands for:

- **Integrity**
- **Needs**
- **Wants**

Developed by Thomas Leonard and his team at Coach U,[2] the theory is that we must make choices based firstly on what we feel is right in relation to our own values and standards of behaviour. Everyone will have their own sense of integrity. What feels wrong to you might be perfectly acceptable to someone else. You will know when you are doing something that feels uncomfortable, even if other people behave that way and seem to have no problem with it.

Being in integrity means meeting your personal duties or obligations and living within your personal code of right or wrong. This integrity forms the solid foundation on which the rest of your life rests.

As you choose which ingredients to highlight in your recipe make sure you are in integrity in the way you apply them. All of these ingredients can be manipulative, misleading or misused if taken to extremes or applied with bad intentions.

Once you have made decisions based on behaving with integrity, you can then make decisions based on getting your needs met. As we saw in Chapter 12, it is important to put your own needs first when pursuing success. This is not to say you completely disregard the needs of other people, but that your needs take priority. When you fly by plane, you are always told in an emergency to fit your own oxygen mask first before fitting a mask on your child. This is because you can focus on getting their mask right only if you are breathing freely. And the same is true with needs. If your needs have been met, you can be fully available when other people require your help.

Finally, once you know you are behaving with integrity and have your needs met, you can pursue your wants, whatever they be. Many people go wrong by pursuing their wants first – I want to be the boss, I want to be rich, I only want to work six months of the year, and so on. They may achieve their goals, but may not find the satisfaction they anticipated.

Here are some other questions which may help you create the perfect recipe for success.

WHAT AM I PASSIONATE ABOUT?

At the start of this book, I questioned whether 'passion' really was an ingredient in success. My scepticism was based on the fact that so many successful people cite it as central to their success and yet many struggling entrepreneurs, professionals and artists are incredibly passionate about what they do, but never achieve dizzying heights of success.

Knowing what you are passionate about entails knowing yourself deeply. And while that isn't enough on its own, having a clear understanding of who you are, why you react the way you do and what 'feeds' you is key to enjoying any success you do have.

Randy Komisar, who describes himself as a 'virtual CEO', has had a career based almost entirely on his passion. He now works with top Silicon Valley companies advising them on strategy and growth. But he has chosen jobs which intrigued him rather than jobs that took him in a particular direction. He has trusted his gut, made decisions based on his friendships with people and let go of the need to impress family and colleagues with his job titles. In his article 'Goodbye Career, Hello Success' he describes the value of being motivated by a passion:

First, it is never dull. Scary, yes. Confounding, often. But boring, never. You're always learning about yourself, other people and the world, and that feels terrific. It feels meaning-ful. Second, a passion-driven career is good for the compa-nies you work for because you're there for the love of the work. You can feel some satisfaction from giving your all to an organisation. Third, a passion-driven career with all its fluidity and flexibility actually happens to make sense in the ever-changing landscape of the new economy. But the best thing about a career like mine is that it isn't a career at all. It's a life.[3]

Most successful people did not fully envision where they are today when they started out. Richard Branson did not know what his port-folio of businesses would look like when he started working for himself in the basement of his family's home. Bill Gates didn't know where his technology would take him. J. K. Rowling may have known where her characters would end up but she didn't know what life had in store for her when she sat down to write the Harry Potter novels.

What they were able to do was follow their passion. As long as they cared about what they were doing, they could sustain them-selves through the difficult times and stay focused on what was important to them.

HOW WELL DO I KNOW MYSELF?

Most successful people who are still enjoying their success are very self-aware, whether they have done this through conscious introspec-tion or not. Through understanding their strengths and weaknesses, their purpose, their values, their motivations and how they respond in different situations, they know themselves very deeply.

Without self-awareness it is still possible to make it to the top, but once there an individual can be very damaged . . . and damaging.

In his 2004 *Harvard Business Review* article on the subject, William George argues that those who have made it to the top of the greasy pole through aggression and determination can do more harm than good once they've reached their goal. Having neglected to spend any time on personal development, they have no authentic personal 'style' and often ape the professional behaviour of others. In the extreme, those who are – in George's words – driven to achieve by short-comings in their character', can be tempted to:

> . . . take inordinate risks on behalf of the organisation. They may even come to believe they are so important that they place their interests above those of the organisation

He concludes that:

> It is only through a deep self-awareness that you can find your inner voice and listen to it.[4]

Successful people may admire other people but they do not want to *be* them: they want to be the best version of themselves they can be. They allow their personality through and it imprints itself on everything they touch: it filters through their team or their organisation, it sits between the lines in the books they write, it is in their poetry or their music.

Knowing what makes you different is the first step to turning that difference in to the quality that makes you special. Hiding what makes you stand out from the crowd, or not even knowing what it is, will massively impair your ability to succeed.

Knowing the impact you have on others is a big part of self-awareness, so this isn't an excuse to run wild and insult, upset or hurt those around you because you are determined to 'be yourself'. But it does mean you can be true to yourself when called upon to make decisions. And it means you will gain satisfaction from the process of achieving success rather than hoping that, when you arrive at your destination, it is as good as you imagined.

WHAT IS MY UNIQUE PATH?

The traditional idea of a career path has been undermined over the last 30 years. While previous generations may have been able to predict the steps it took to get to the top in their field, it is not so simple today. Some people make it to the top in one single leap and are multi-millionaires by the time they are 29 years old. Others zig-zag from one seemingly unrelated experience to another. Still others manage three or four serious careers in one lifetime, excelling at each one.

And you can start any time. It used to be that decisions you made about the subjects you were going to study at school determined the rest of your life. Whether you dropped sciences or languages at the age of 14 seemed absolutely crucial, as did deciding whether to go to university and what to study.

Today, the situation is less clear. More youngsters go into further education than ever before and yet many of our most respected success icons did not have a conventional education. I know many professionals who spent 20 years in the corporate world as middle managers and only in their 40s or 50s did they pursue a lifelong ambition and turn it in to a massive success.

Clearly there is no longer one guaranteed route to success. This makes it easier in some ways and more difficult in others. It is more difficult because you cannot simply sign on the dotted line at a recruit-ment fair and, 30 years later, find yourself at the top. You have to be more conscious of your choices. Your company may commit to your ongoing development by investing in leadership training and team bonding excursions, but there are no guaranteed promotions based on years in service. Those who get ahead have worked for it, employ-ing the ingredients outlined in this book. Those who don't work at it get stuck in one place.

However, it is easier now that the rules have been eroded in that, if you are determined enough, you can never reach a dead end. You can still be looking for your dream job, your big break or your revolu-tionary new invention in your 30s, 40s, 50s and beyond. There never comes a point where you have to accept you are average in every way. Of course, you may need to dramatically change direction, be willing to start from scratch or take a gamble in order to continue in your pursuit of excellence. You may have always wanted to make it as a singer but discover after your fourth X-Factor audition that you really couldn't carry a tune in a bucket. But you may still have huge success as a producer, a promoter or a presenter. In the past due to lack of education, social background or simply a face that didn't fit, you could have found yourself never achieving your full potential. Today, in our society, there really is no excuse.

Designing your own path means setting out on a route that seems most likely to take you to the goals that matter to you and then tacking and jiving throughout your life depending on the opportunities that come your way (or the opportunities that you create). It means keeping your eyes open, never becoming complacent, never relying on other people to hand you success on a plate. It means keeping on keeping on even when some people question your choices or argue that you are making life hard for yourself.

DO I ACCEPT MYSELF?

Success isn't for everyone. Actually, let me rephrase that. Everyone has it in them to reach the top in some area. It might not be the area in which you currently imagine yourself reaching the top. You may be on the wrong path for you and only discover this when you are further down the line. But I truly believe everyone has what it takes to be successful at something.

But would you want to? The kind of success I have been describing – making it to the top of the field – isn't all it is cracked up to be. Not only is it a never-ending journey but using all ten key ingredients simultaneously is hard work. You must:

- **Remember your manners**
- **Stay focused**

- Have nerves of steel
- Gain trust
- Surround yourself with trusted advisers and supporters
- Play the politics game
- Hone your talent
- Keep pushing yourself beyond your original goals
- Be inventive
- . . . and knuckle down

You may have to compromise on your personal life or your personal life may have to adapt a great deal to you. Your partner may need to be willing to sacrifice his or her own career or accept they will see little of you. Your children may have to get used to you not being around. Your friends may describe you as someone who is always late or always calls to cancel. And you have to feel that none of this is as important as what you are working on, or that the price being paid now is a small one compared with the prize being offered later on.

For many people it is a no-brainer. They know what they want and they know it is worth it to them. For others, it is a battle they get drawn in to based on the expectations of others, their need to compete or unresolved issues from the past which leave them feeling they have to prove something to someone.

If you don't believe you can behave with integrity and follow this recipe, then success of the kind we have been talking about might not result in a fulfilling life for you. If deep down you don't care that much about this kind of success but measure success more by the way you spend your time outside of work, it is as well to know now. By ignoring the truth you simply set up false expectations and are a constant disappointment to yourself and others.

However, if through understanding these ingredients you realise that you have what it takes and following the recipe would not feel like a high price to pay, then throw yourself in to it without regret. Healthy successful people take personal responsibility for the choices they have made and do not blame other people. They find a balance that suits them. It may not be working nine-to-five and spending the weekends playing football at the park, and their choices might look like madness to other people. But they know what balance feels right for them and they commit to achieving it. And maybe, as leadership psychologist Manfred F. R. Kets de Vries puts it, it helps to be a little mad:

> I happen to believe that those who accept the madness in themselves may be the healthiest leaders of all.[5]

If, as a result of reading this book, you have decided that your fulfil-ment will come from balancing all the areas of your life – work you enjoy and a life outside which meets your other needs – then I wish you well. This is a liberating realisation and one which, I hope, you are able to pursue with vigour and commitment.

If, on the other hand, you feel confident you can mix up these ingredients in to your own recipe for success, then I commend you for your courage and your tenacity. And I hope above all that you enjoy the journey. As Robert Louis Stevenson wrote:

> To travel hopefully is a better thing than to arrive, and true success is to labour.

REFERENCES

1 Jones, Peter. *Tycoon*. p.253. London: Hodder & Stoughton 2007.
2 www.coachinc.com
3 Komisar, Randy. 'Goodbye Career, Hello Success.' p.2. *Harvard Business Review*, March 2000.
4 George, William. 'Leading by Feel – Finding your Voice'. p.35. *Harvard Business Review* January 2004.
5 Coutu, Diane L. 'Putting Leaders on the Couch: Manfred F. R. Kets de Vries'. p.71. *Harvard Business Review*, January 2004.

Index